Scarlett MccGwire is an author and freelance journalist. She was part of the first jobshare President of any trade union when she was President of the National Union of Journalists. She has written two other books, *Kim's Story - A Fight for Life* and *Transforming Moments*. She lives in north London with journalist Christian Wolmar and their assortment of children, Molly, Pascoe and Misha.

Best Companies for Women

SCARLETT MCGWIRE

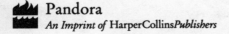

Pandora
An Imprint of HarperCollins*Publishers*

Pandora Press
An Imprint of Harper Collins*Publishers*
77-85 Fulham Palace Road
London W6 8JB

Published by Pandora Press in 1992
10 9 8 7 6 5 4 3 2 1

A CIP record for this book
is available from the British Library.

ISBN 0 04 440697 5

Typeset by Harper Phototypesetters Limited,
Northampton, England
Printed in Great Britain by
HarperCollinsManufacturing Glasgow

To Christian, with all my love.

To
New Directions Network.
Many thanks for all
your help & support.

Best wishes

Sue Moss

April 1995

CONTENTS

Acknowledgements *11*

PART 1

The Best Companies *20*; Why Companies Need Equal
Opportunities Policies *23*; Recruiting Women *26*; Does Age
Matter? *27*; Maternity Leave *29*; Career Breaks *31*; What
Are Companies Offering For Women Who Want to Return
After Having Children? *31*; Part-time Working *32*;
Jobsharing *34*; Term-time Working *34*; Working From Home
35; Workplace Nurseries *35*; Promotion *37*; Training *40*;
Targeting *41*; What Makes a Company Good for Women? *43*;
Using Part 2 *43*.

PART 2   The 50 Best Companies

Councils

Cambridge City Council *47*; Edinburgh District Council *51*;
Gloucestershire County Council *54*; Leicester City Council
58; London Borough of Islington *62*; Oxfordshire County
Council *66*; Sheffield City Council *69*.

Engineering

British Aerospace *73*; Brown & Root (UK) Ltd *77*; General
Electric Company *81*; Lucas Industries plc *85*; Ove Arup *89*;
Rover Group *92*.

Finance

Alliance & Leicester Building Society *96*; Barclays Bank *100*;
Halifax Building Society *104*; Legal & General *107*; Midland
Bank *111*; National Westminster Bank PLC *115*; Prudential

Corporation *118*; Royal Bank of Scotland *121*; Sun Life of Canada *124*; TSB *128*.

High-Tech

Bull HN Information Systems Ltd *131*; International Computers Ltd (ICL) *135*; Rank Xerox *139*.

Manufacturing

Imperial Chemical Industries (ICI) *142*; Mars *146*; Smith's *149*.

Media

BBC *152*; Channel Four *157*; London Weekend Television *161*; Research & Development Services (RDS) *165*; Thames Television *168*; Yorkshire Television *172*.

Oil Companies

British Petroleum Company plc (BP) *176*; Esso *180*; Shell UK Ltd *184*.

Public and Private Services

The British Council *188*; British Rail *192*; British Telecom *196*; The Civil Service *200*; NALGO *204*; National Health Service *207*; Croyden District Health Authority *210*.

Retail

Boots the Chemists *213*; Littlewoods *217*; Marks & Spencer *220*; Sainsbury's *224*.

Voluntary Organisations

Oxfam *228*; Save The Children Fund *232*.

PART 3

Honourable Mentions *239*; Companies Which Have Equal Opportunities Recruitment *248*; Companies Which are Taking Action to Get More Women into Management or into Male-dominated Technical Areas *250*; Companies Which Run Women-only Training *251*; Companies Which Provide Health Care *253*; Companies With Policies on Sexual Harassment *255*; Companies With Maternity Provision Above the Statutory Minimum *256*; Companies With Childcare Provision *259*; Companies With Flexible Hours and Conditions on Return From Maternity Leave *261*; Legal Rights *266*.

ACKNOWLEDGEMENTS

Many people have helped me with this book. For every company I have written up there was at least one person who supplied me with all the information, dealt with all my queries and put me in touch with women to interview. For the most part they do not appear in the book and I would like to thank all of them for the work they put in, particularly those who had to delicately negotiate with their senior management for me to be allowed the information I needed. Without their unsung hard work this book would never have been completed.

I am extraordinarily grateful to my agent, Jane Gregory, for coming up with the idea, and my editors Philippa Brewster and Ginny Iliff, who somehow managed that mixture of patience, tolerance, encouragement and toughness that kept me writing to the end. Barbara Gunnell helped me develop the idea, and Sally Gilbert has given a lot of advice and criticism but bears no responsibility for any of the ideas. Pilli Valdez looked after the children, Molly, Pascoe and Misha, who while they might not have helped certainly ensured I did not feel lonely at my desk. Above all, my thanks to Christian Wolmar who not only read it all, at every stage, but put up with me as I wrote it.

PART 1

'The business world's bias against women is so longstanding and so deeply ingrained that waiting for the current glacial pace of change to take its course wastes a potential resource and condemns too many aspiring business women to unfair struggles. British businesses should take positive action to employ the skills and talents of half of the population that is usually neglected.'

Management Today, 1988.

While I was writing this book a friend asked me what I was going to call it. When I told her she laughed and said, 'Well, that will be a short book.'

During the writing and researching of *Best Companies for Women* I have blown hot and cold about whether effective efforts are being made to adapt companies to the needs of women instead of women always adapting themselves to the needs of companies. I must stress that I have only looked at the companies which are doing something – the top 500; the rest of British employers still belong firmly in the Dark Ages.

On the one hand a lot is being done by the better companies to cater for the needs of mothers. The workplace nursery, so loved by the media, is far from universal, but as the list on page 259 shows, more companies than I expected do have them. A number of organisations offer reduced hours of work to women following their return from maternity leave, and the most progressive ones have a whole range of flexible options to offer, including career breaks. These may consist of a break of up to a few years while the children are young; the opportunity to work from home; and flexible hours negotiated with the individual to suit her circumstances. In the better companies, these maternity packages apply to all women, which is an advance on the old days when part-time was only for lowly paid women. Now women managers are entitled to see their children as well as pursue their careers.

However, the problems that women have always encountered –

in achieving their potential and in climbing the career ladder as fast as men are able to - are still very much with us. Members of most boards of most companies are still all male, and all of them are white. The percentage of women in senior management is tiny, even in industries where women make up most of the workforce, like finance and retail. Many reasons, and some excuses, are given for this state of affairs, but the fact remains that in the 1990s, in what is laughingly called the post-feminist era, women are still having difficulty in achieving for themselves basic equality with their male colleagues at work. It is far easier for companies to deal with the demands motherhood makes on women, by instituting flexible hours, career breaks, enhanced maternity breaks or even workplace nurseries, than to deal with the very real problem that women are not getting promoted in any great numbers.

One of the great barriers to promotion for women is the long hours that management, and more particularly senior management, are required to put in. Throughout this book women note that people are rewarded for the hours they put in rather than for their achievement. This is not a matter, they say, of only working late during crises; people are given jobs which cannot be completed in less than sixty hours a week. Such long hours are particularly punitive for women with children, who are torn between the demands of their offspring and those of their work, but women without children, too, have commitments, and a life to lead outside work. Companies need to wake up to the fact that people work more efficiently in shorter bursts over reasonable hours - working most evenings as well as weekends does not lead to innovative decisions - and women are beginning to prove their point in practice, performing quickly and efficiently over reasonable working days.

This book is not a study on the problems of mixing children with careers; it does not examine why some women return successfully and others do not, and how tough it is for the seemingly successful ones. Instead, it focuses on how some companies have made it easier or, in some cases, possible for women to combine a career with children. The women who speak in this book are the ones who have managed that difficult juggling act. They bear witness to how tough it is. Many of them bring work home with them so that they can see their children before they go to bed, they then work at home for the rest of the evening. Their stamina is amazing – I do not know how they do it. Throughout the book I am talking about the problems of mothers rather than of parents. While I believe that fathers should take as much responsibility for childcare as mothers, and would transform the working environment if they did, unfortunately the vast majority of mothers are left to do the juggling, and it is they who need the flexible hours, career breaks and workplace nurseries. As Barbara Brown, Personnel Manager of the engineering firm Brown & Root, says: 'The key to being a successful working mother is choosing the right father.'

For the white woman in her twenties and thirties, working life is certainly looking up. For her sisters from the ethnic minorities, life is still tough, although companies with the best policies on gender are the most likely ones to be implementing positive policies for ethnic minorities. Most of the women interviewed in this book are white because Black people are still a rarity in management. Most of the people featured here are also in their twenties and thirties: they are the people who are benefiting from the changes. For the older women under the old regimes it was tough and progress was slow. Where are they now?

For the most part the companies which are implementing progressive policies have only started to adopt them quite recently. Littlewoods, which is probably the pioneer, has been practising equal opportunities for twenty-five years. But even the large clearing banks and the Civil Service, which are looked on by many as a benchmark, only started in the early 1980s, while a few of the companies I have profiled in Part 2 are only just beginning to put action plans into practice, for example the engineering firm Lucas, and TSB.

Over recent years new pressures have been developing in companies to improve their policies on women. One of these is the demographic time bomb, whereby because of the fall in the birth rate since the 1970s there are now far fewer school leavers every year. The demographic time bomb has concentrated the minds of company powers that be to think differently about recruitment. One new target for recruitment is women who have left work to have children and would like to return. Companies have asked themselves how they might encourage such women to come back to work, and are now offering them flexible hours or jobshares to make it easier for them to combine motherhood and work.

The skills shortage is another incentive for companies to take the recruitment of women seriously. This lack of trained people in the UK applies particularly to engineers, but there is also a shortage of people with most practical skills. As companies fight to get the best people for the job, particularly among skilled graduates, women are now in as much demand as men. However, in order to keep a skilled woman, so that her training benefits her employers throughout her career, they necessarily must deal with the likelihood that she will have children and will therefore be presented with potentially conflicting responsibilities: her career and the upbringing of her children.

Factors like these have led many of the better companies to understand that proper equal opportunities make good business sense. Recruiting and training staff is an expensive business. Keeping good women with the company, and fully using their skills and potential rather than having to recruit and retrain their successors, makes economic sense. All the commercial companies I spoke to agreed that their equal opportunity policies paid for themselves in both attracting applicants of higher calibre and keeping them. During uncertain times of economic decline it is particularly important that equal opportunity policies are not abandoned: keeping people on saves companies money.

Women themselves are encouraging companies to think of women in their policy-making. Many of the women I interviewed would not call themselves feminists, but all of them have felt the effects of the Women's Movement of the 1970s and 1980s, and they demonstrate in this book that they take it for granted that they are as capable as their male colleagues, if not more so. They expect equal treatment and they do not expect to have to choose between their children and their careers. The trade unions too have been battling for women's rights for years, and while only the Save The Children Fund was brave enough to put up a shop steward for me to interview for their profile, many of those initiatives for which managements are taking the credit have been argued for by trade unionists year after year.

So the news for women who are looking for new challenges and new employment possibilities, or just a job that allows motherhood to be compatible with a career, is that things are looking up, and that the better companies are slowly, often reluctantly, but increasingly opening their doors to them. How did this author discover which companies are doing so most effectively, finding fifty to concentrate on in detail out of so many?

I selected the companies on the basis of their answers to questionnaires covering these various policy areas concerning women: the proportion of women employed and in management; promotion policy; training – in particular women-only training; maternity leave and pay, and provisions for returning from a maternity break, such as reduced hours and workplace nurseries; policy on sexual harassment; and policy on health, such as on smoking or cancer screening. I widened the definition of companies to include the public and voluntary sector as large numbers of women choose to work in these sectors, often because they are willing to sacrifice pay for the better working conditions which have long been available in the public sector.

I assessed the answers to the questionnaire on a sector by sector basis: it seemed unfair to judge an engineering company employing very few women, for instance, against a retail or finance company that might have a workforce of which 80 per cent are women. Since each company was judged against others in its own sector, it was much more difficult to get a place in this book as a local authority or finance or retail company than as an engineering or manufacturing company. Many organisations in the first group are doing a great deal for women, whilst in the second few organisations are trying to attract women.

Finally, I had succeeded in finding fifty companies which can be said to be good employers. I wanted to talk with at least three women from each one, to find out about their experiences and thus how policy was actually put into practice. At least one woman in each company who spoke to me was a mother with young children. These women were chosen, for the most part, by the companies but, as you can see in Part 2, few felt it necessary to toe a company line. I am sure that most of the compliments they gave to their employers are genuine, but those companies which do come in for criticism from their women staff can still gain credit for being places where people are able to speak freely.

Each of these women provides the reader with a rare inside view of what it is like working for a particular company in a particular job. Together they give us an insight into the lives and experiences of white collar women working today. They voice their expectation that they be recognised and treated according to their merits rather than their gender – this above all can be commonly and clearly heard in the pages that follow.

THE BEST COMPANIES

The end results were fascinating and often unexpected. Overall the Civil Service comes out on top, not because each of its policies is better than any other company but because it offers women such a comprehensive range. The Civil Service has been looking at equal opportunities for over a decade, trying to ensure that good women are recruited, that they make progress and are not held back if they become parents. The third most senior person at the Department of the Environment, the Under Secretary, Diane Phillips, is on a four-day week – proof that one can get to the top and still have a life outside work. Other companies please note.

Talking to women in the Civil Service helped to clear my mind of prejudices that I had held about it being a stuffy, paper-pushing organisation. How ironic, then, that throughout the 1980s, when we had a government which militated against working women and allowed provisions for working mothers to fall well below those of our partners in the European Community, its arm, the Civil Service, made enormous strides to try to make sure its female staff are treated fairly.

Predictably perhaps, the retail and finance sectors have done extremely well. Here are companies which traditionally employ a lot of women and have high turnovers of staff. These are the companies most affected by the demographic time bomb and they are looking to employ many more working mothers. Boots The Chemist, for example, has pioneered term-time contracts for women who want to fit their work around their children's school hours and take the school holidays off.

The best retail and finance companies are not merely trying to
recruit mothers as well as school leavers; they are encouraging
women to progress in their organisations. Sainsbury's has
instituted a junior management position of Section Manager,
ensuring that progress can thus be made from the shop floor
through to management. All Section Managers can work part-
time, opening these positions to people with domestic
commitments. Like Sainsbury's, many banks, among them the
Midland, National Westminster, Barclays and the Royal Bank of
Scotland, have Equal Opportunity Managers who have
established firm policies against discrimination, slowly changing
their companies' profiles from the conventional one – men at the
top of the hierarchy and women at the bottom – to more of a
gender mix all the way through.

Local authorities, also as I had expected, did well. It is
interesting to observe that many schemes pioneered by left-wing
Labour controlled councils and pilloried in the popular press as
a waste of money, like women-only courses and codes on sexual
harassment, have been happily taken up by commercial
companies. The policies of a council like Islington in north London,
are unquestionably politically motivated, and the councillors
brought in a policy of allowing all women to benefit from their
generous maternity provisions without having to have worked a
qualifying period for the council; they did so partly out of a sense
of fairness. The life assurance company Legal & General has
adopted the same policy as Islington, but they justify their
initiative purely on commercial grounds: when we hire a person,
the company says, this is a long-term commitment because he or
she is right for the job, and a break for maternity does not alter
that fact.

The problem with having equal opportunities as part of a
political agenda is that in the harsh atmosphere of the 1990s, when
the implementation of the poll tax and strict government rules on
spending has meant that councils are desperate to make savings,
an equal opportunities policy risks being viewed as a luxury rather
than the cost effective measure it is known to be in commercial
companies. Leicester City Council's policy to make all posts open
to jobsharers has helped to ease its recruitment difficulties. It is,

for instance, difficult to recruit planners wherever you are in the UK, but Leicester has a jobsharing partnership of two women Planners who applied to the council because of its jobsharing policy. A Personnel Officer was offered a much higher-paid job elsewhere but stayed with Leicester because she had a baby and felt it would be easier to combine motherhood and career working for the council. Again, this can be given as evidence that equal opportunities do save money.

It is certainly not just Labour-run authorities which are good for women. Both Oxfordshire and Gloucestershire County Councils, which have no political party in overall control, are excellent for women.

An interesting group to survey is the media. Newspapers, magazines and book publishers barely get a mention in here, but there are five television companies, including the BBC, that do. Recruitment has never been a problem in television, people are banging on the doors to get in, yet Thames and London Weekend Television had crèche places long before they became part of a fashionable agenda.

The most surprising group of all is the oil industry. This is unquestionably traditional and male dominated, yet BP, Shell and Esso have gone to unusual lengths to make their companies more women-friendly. The recruitment among science graduates is up to 50 per cent women and 50 per cent men in some areas. There is a particular shortage of engineers and scientists: the oil companies are doing their best to attract the young women as well as the young men coming out of university, and there are numbers of successful young women in middle management within the companies. There are enhanced benefits for new mothers – six months fully paid leave with Shell, for instance, and part-time working on returning to work. These initiatives are relatively recent so it will take time to see if these women can get into senior management in sufficient numbers to make it usual for a woman to reach the top, instead of extremely unusual as it is at the moment.

Not enough engineers are being trained to meet the needs of the engineering companies, so the more progressive ones like British Aerospace and GEC are going into the schools to persuade students to consider engineering as a career. Both these companies target girls and send women as well as men to make the presentations. There are still very few women working in engineering, and even the companies mentioned in the book, with the exception of Ove Arup and Rover, do not do very much for women engineers. However, this is changing – all the companies are beginning to act. Lucas has set the tone by hiring, at a senior level, an Equal Opportunities Manager to put policy into practice.

WHY COMPANIES NEED EQUAL OPPORTUNITIES POLICIES

Good employers do not happen by accident. The companies in which women thrive have well thought out equal opportunities policies. Discrimination is so deeply ingrained in British employment that it occurs unthinkingly. Jobs are often thought of as women's jobs or men's jobs, with the woman's job having lower status. In many firms the fact that women have children makes them a liability and often a short-term prospect. Women are often considered emotionally unsuitable for certain work, ranging from supervising people and dealing with technical equipment through to making important decisions rationally. All this is, of course, blind prejudice in the face of evidence which shows that women are as efficient and effective as men. However, a company which has not examined its prejudices still acts on them.

The temptation is ever there to recruit and promote staff in one's own image. It takes effort to look at skills and achievements objectively, following the needs of the organisation rather than one's own prejudices. As long as any demands children make on working mothers are seen as detrimental to the company and the woman's achievements, most women's careers will go into a decline when they start to have children.

An equal opportunities policy might merely be a few lines stating that all employees are treated the same regardless of gender, race or creed. This is a small first step towards fair employment practices, but a vital one. The better companies have policies which express far more than good intentions and go on to spell out guidelines in the recruitment, promotion and treatment of staff.

Those companies which do not have a policy because they maintain that naturally all employees are treated as individuals, as some told me when I asked about their policies, do nevertheless naturally discriminate despite their good intentions. Unfortunately, it is 'natural' to discriminate against women, it takes thought and effort not to do so.

Richard Sherrard, the Equal Opportunities Manager of the Halifax Building Society, has a clear philosophy: 'I believe all people are different and you have to accept the differences and develop policies so the differences don't disadvantage people, so women who have babies are not disadvantaged.'

Only one of the chosen top fifty companies in this book has no equal opportunities policy: Research & Development Services. This is because it is a small company, employing only twenty-six people, of whom twenty-one are women. Even so, the company is looking to develop a solid policy rather than merely *ad hoc* arrangements to suit individual needs.

Equal opportunities policies are steps in the right direction but sadly they do not solve the problem of discrimination. Mr Sherrard from the Halifax said that after 130 years without a policy, the introduction of one did not transform the Halifax. However, 'it formalised the fact that we want to develop fair employment practices'.

A 1988 British Institute of Management survey of 350 member organisations showed that though some organisations had some commitment to equal opportunities, less than a third were taking active steps to ensure they were being put into practice:

- 51 per cent had an equal opportunities policy and a senior executive with responsibility for equal opportunities
- 59 per cent had announced a commitment to equal opportunities policies at board level
- 35 per cent examined their practices and procedures at least once a year to try to ensure a lack of discrimination
- 28 per cent had announced a commitment to equal opportunities in collective agreements.

Women and Men in Britain, published by the Equal
Opportunities Commission in 1989, stated that:

- Women made up 40 per cent of the labour force and their share is
  expected to increase to 44 per cent by the end of the century
- The number of young people is expected to fall by 1.4 million
  between 1987 and 2000
- 90 per cent of men are economically active between their mid-
  twenties and their mid-fifties; 70 per cent of women are similarly
  active during this time but the proportion fluctuates as many
  women in their mid-twenties and early thirties temporarily withdraw
  from the labour market to bring up children
- Most men work full-time while half the married women and a
  quarter of the non-married women work part-time
- 12.5 per cent of people in employment are self-employed; 75 per
  cent of these are male. Almost all self-employed men work full-time
  but more than half of self-employed married women work
  part-time.
- Young women in full-time jobs and on youth training schemes (YTS)
  are concentrated in traditionally female occupations, such as clerical
  work, selling, catering, cleaning, hairdressing and other personal
  services
- By 1995 20 per cent of managers and entrepreneurs are expected
  to be women, although compared to their overall share of
  employment women will still remain under-represented in these
  occupations
- By 1995 80 per cent of clerical and secretarial workers and 70 per
  cent in sales and personal service occupations, are likely to be
  women
- One worker in 13 in construction and one in 7 in primary industries
  and utilities are women, while more women than men are employed
  in non-market services, a sector which includes health services,
  education and public administration. By 1995 the non-marketed
  services sector is expected to account for almost 30 per cent of
  female employment.
- Women graduates are four times more likely than men to take up
  employment as teachers or lecturers.

Unfortunately, many companies with an equal opportunities policy think a paragraph of good intention is enough. They have few other policies which make any efforts to achieve any equality whatsoever. Liberal sentiment is supposed to win the day.

When applying for a job it is worth looking at the company's equal opportunities policy. It can help to show you how serious the company is in its dealings with women. Watch for fine words which are really only lip service to fine feelings. The policies that go on to deal with action about recruitment, training, promotion and encouraging women to return after having children, are taking the issues for women employees seriously. An equal opportunities policy combined with an action plan are the keys to knowing that here is a good company.

RECRUITING WOMEN

To start at the beginning: many companies say that their greatest problem is getting women to apply for jobs, particularly in non-traditional areas like sales or engineering. There are, however, positive strategies that may encourage more women applicants. For example, Mars decided they needed women engineers and put an advertisement in the *Sunday Times* specifically inviting applications from women. This was extraordinarily successful: not only did more women reply than had ever replied to an advertisement before, but more men did as well, possibly because such an unusual event made the company more interesting. Mars did not need to advertise again that year. The company also found that on the whole the female applicants were much better qualified than the male ones, and that they were more inclined to be apologetic at having the temerity to apply.

Many companies have looked closely at their recruitment procedures to get rid of assumptions that might prejudice women. Why should a mother be asked about childcare arrangements and not a father? Why should a young woman be asked whether she plans to have a baby and a young man not asked about his plans for fatherhood? Why should the question be asked at all? It is unfortunately true that these sorts of questions are still being asked during job interviews. If this does happen it can be taken as a clear indication that the company does not take equal opportunities seriously.

The first step in recruitment should be to look at the job which the person has left and then at what the company needs the job to be, and to draw up what is called a person specification, which lists the skills and qualities an applicant will need. Interviewers should not have an idea of the person wanted to fill the job but the skills needed. The Civil Service and many councils insist on always having a woman on an interviewing panel.

Training recruiters in equal opportunities is not just an altruistic exercise on behalf of women and Black people, it means that it is more likely that the best person for the job will be hired rather than a face that fits. As long as a woman has to prove herself to be better than a man to get work, companies are missing out on a lot of female talent.

Richard Sherrard of the Halifax Building Society believes the key to a good business is good recruitment: 'If we get the selection right, attracting the people who will do the job right, they will bring the right performance. Having the right people with the right skills in the right job justifies any expense of an equal opportunities policy. When you get the wrong people, it is very expensive. If equal opportunities is inherent then it saves you a lot of money.'

DOES AGE MATTER?

I wish I could say that age does not matter and there is no prejudice against older people, but depressingly this turned out to be the case. If you are over 40 and job hunting, whether you are male or female, you will not find much encouragement in the recruitment policies of many companies in Britain.

Some companies, however, do take account of the issues surrounding age within their equal opportunities policies, and most of the companies profiled here do say either that there is no age limit in recruitment or that anyone up to the age of 63 - two years short of retirement - will be considered as an applicant. In practice, it is tough getting a good job if you are over the age of 40, particularly if you are female.

Of course there are exceptions. In this book there are two women who were recruited when they were over 40, one to the Civil Service, the other to British Rail. A Senior Personnel Manager was recruited to GEC in her forties, however she told me that GEC had been one of the few companies she could even apply to because most of the advertisements in her trade paper, which is published by the Institute of Personnel Management, had an upper age limit of 40, even though the institute's employment policy specifically states that companies should not discriminate on the grounds of age.

A 1989 survey by the company MSL showed that of 1,284 executive or management posts advertised, 86.6 per cent had an upper age limit of 40. For those over 45 there were fewer jobs on offer in most sectors than there were in 1987: 3.1 per cent were willing to recruit people over 45, 0.6 per cent those over 50.

The companies which have gained publicity because they are actively recruiting older people, like Tesco and the do-it-yourself chain B & Q, tend to be offering shopfloor jobs normally given to school leavers. The same is true of the flexible contracts for workers over 55 offered by Thistle Hotels. British Telecom, however, has extended the upper age limit of its apprentice scheme by twenty-two years, from 19 to 41.

Unquestionably age discrimination militates against women more than men. Women often take longer to become qualified and they may take years out of the job market to rear children. Instead of being welcomed back into employment, they are often treated as if they are over the hill. Of course they are not - experience hard won does not vanish beneath the burdens of childcare.

During 1988 and 1989 the Commons' Employment Select Committee did look at the employment patterns of the over fifties. The committee was so disturbed at its findings that it suggested to the Trade Union Congress and Confederation of British Industry that they should mount a joint campaign to challenge discrimination against older workers. The employment service, it said, should always ask employers seeking to impose age restrictions on recruitment if they are strictly necessary.

A campaign to ban ageism in recruitment has been launched by the Alliance Against Ageism. The campaign will focus on the need for legislation to outlaw the use of upper age limits in recruitment advertising. The Alliance comprises a number of organisations working against age discrimination in employment and promoting older workers. Member organisations include Age Concern England, the Campaign Against Age Discrimination in Employment, Grey Matters and Help the Aged.

The 1980s were a decade when the yuppy ruled and youth was king. Perhaps in the 1990s some cognizance will be taken of age and experience.

MATERNITY LEAVE

When Geoff Smith from the Legal & General was looking at what the company could do to improve maternity benefits, he was shocked at how low the statutory minimum was: 'I don't know how women manage on it.'

Women who have been with their employer for at least two years at the beginning of the eleventh week before the baby is due are entitled to six weeks' paid maternity leave at 90 per cent of their weekly wage, and twelve weeks at what is called lower rate Statutory Maternity Pay which, on 1 April 1991, was £44.50 per week. They are also entitled to take up to twenty-nine weeks off after the birth.

Increasingly the better companies agree with Geoff Smith and many offer much better deals to their female staff than this statutory minimum. Interestingly, the better the benefits the more likely women are to return to work.

The two-year qualification period has been shortened by many companies and some, like the Legal & General and local councils such as Camden, Islington, Brighton, Bristol and Cambridge, have no qualification at all – a woman may join pregnant and still be entitled to full maternity benefit.

Longer maternity leave, both paid and unpaid, is offered by some of the better companies, so women are not bounced into coming back but feel more ready to return and are more likely to stay when they do. Most local authorities and the Civil Service offer up to a year off, not all of it paid.

The more progressive companies give extra maternity pay

which is sometimes dependent on the mother returning to work.
Some, like British Telecom, withhold the extra until after the
return to work; others like Islington Council expect part of the
extra to be repaid if there is no return.

---

*The numbers of women returning to work in 1989 after having
a baby increased dramatically according, to a study entitled*
Maternity Rights: The Experience of Women and Employers,
First Findings *by S. McRae and W. W. Daniel, published by the
Policy Studies Institute.*

*Nearly half of the women who were in work when they
became pregnant returned to their jobs within nine months of
the baby's birth, compared with only a quarter in 1979. They
are also more likely to return to full-time rather than part-time
work.*

*The study found striking inequality between the private and
the public sector. Women in the public sector are twice as likely
to continue in paid work following the baby's birth, and the
public sector does more to encourage mothers to return. The
contrast is particularly marked in relation to provisions such
as flexi-time, jobsharing, career breaks and workplace childcare
facilities. Public employers are also more likely to take up
maternity provisions that go beyond the statutory minimum,
such as extended periods of maternity leave and increased
rates of maternity pay.*

---

*The Industrial Relations Services Maternity Survey in May
1989 of 120 employers showed the average return to work rate
of women covered by these agreements was almost twice that of
women who do not benefit from additional maternity pay or
leave (49 per cent compared to 25.4 per cent).*

CAREER BREAKS

In addition to maternity leave, women may want to take time out to look after their children as they grow up. A growing number of good companies have what are called career breaks, which allow parents to take a few years out to look after children, or in some cases to look after elderly relatives, and have a guaranteed job when they return. Career Break Schemes began in the early 1980s in the large clearing banks. They provided a total break from work for childcare for up to five years and were strictly limited to high-flying women. Over the decade they changed considerably, they became more flexible and more widely available to women lower down the career structure. In the best companies they are becoming part of a totally flexible approach to working, so a woman can either take some time off or work on some sort of part-time basis, whichever suits her. Sainsbury's career break scheme can be a total break of up to five years; or part-time work during that period is also available, as it is with Barclays Bank and the Midland. To qualify for most schemes the woman must have a satisfactory work record. Some of the companies offering career breaks still offer a better deal to management and highly-skilled women than to lower grade staff, but increasingly the same terms are open to all women.

Lesley Holland, the former Equal Opportunities Manager of British Rail, another pioneer of the Career Break Scheme, says the chances of women reaching senior levels in their organisation have grown enormously because of these schemes.

WHAT ARE COMPANIES OFFERING FOR WOMEN WHO WANT TO RETURN AFTER HAVING CHILDREN?

The Maternity Alliance published a survey of 250 women in March 1989 which looked at what factors affect their readiness to return to work after having a child. *Women, Work and Maternity: The Inside Story* by Frances O'Grady and Heather Wakefield found that the main factors were:

▌ time off for child sickness

▌ the right to return to old job
▌ flexible working hours
▌ the right to return part-time.

The *Industrial Relations Review and Report Maternity Survey*
looked at 120 organisations employing over one million people in
June 1989. Only thirty-six organisations allowed women to work
part-time or jobshare when they returned from maternity leave,
and for eight of those it was a temporary arrangement. Yet the
survey found that organisations offering women with children
reduced working hours have a higher rate of return after
maternity leave than those which do not – 39 per cent as opposed
to 29 per cent.

PART-TIME WORKING

Part-time working used to mean bad rates of pay for semi-skilled
work. Unfortunately, in too many cases, this is still true and
women who can only take on part-time work because of childcare
responsibilities earn a lower hourly rate than full-timers, and are
often not entitled to perks or benefits. A woman working less than
twenty hours a week must work for a company for five years
before she is entitled to maternity benefit, as against the two
years demanded of a full-timer. The European Directive on Part-
time Working states that pay and benefits should be given to part-
timers on a pro rata basis, so they are paid at the same hourly rate
as full-timers and are entitled to a proportion of the benefits. This
recommendation should eventually become law, but already
companies like the Legal & General are discussing implementing
it.

In the best companies, a lot of options are now opening up to
women who do not want to return to work full-time. Their
changing attitudes to part-time working can be explained by the
fact that skilled, high-flying women are demanding a change in
their working hours. These women want to watch their children
growing up and often negotiate flexible hours while on maternity
leave, sometimes on an individual basis but increasingly, among

the better companies, as part of company policy. Most of the women in this book who are on flexible hours made it quite clear that they would only return to work on those hours and otherwise would look elsewhere.

Ideally there should be a range of options on offer to women and men in order to match their working hours to the requirements of the company concerned. In divisions of the Legal & General, and some other companies too, the hours are agreed individually between the employee and the company. At Esso, a senior tax lawyer who is also one of the most senior women in the company, works a three-day week at the moment so that she gets a lot of time with her toddler on her days off; when he starts at school she intends to work five short days.

Increasingly companies are being persuaded to be more imaginative in their response to women's needs, and returning to work after maternity leave, particularly in the south-east of England where the skills shortage is most acute, can be a matter of negotiating hours. This is a possibility that is well worth returners remembering.

The key to part-time working is to match the demands of the job to the needs of the woman. As always, if there is a will at the top of the organisation it is surprising how much can be achieved. The head of London Weekend Television, Greg Dyke, has told his management that if any woman returning after having a baby is refused a request for part-time working he wants the reason in writing: making the ability to work flexible hours the norm rather than the exception.

It is not a one-way process: the company gains as well as the woman. Wendy Mitchell of Research Data Services says the flexibility allowed to the part-timers who work there is more than paid back by the commitment they give to the company. There is no reason why every job needs to be done five days a week and eight (or more) hours a day.

However, women negotiating an individual deal for flexible hours need to ensure that they are covered by the company's union agreement and entitled to all benefits negotiated by the union – if there is a union. If not, they should try to ensure they have as much job security as they had when they were full-time.

JOBSHARING

A jobshare is simply a job done by two people. Normally the hours
are divided in half, either mornings and afternoons or half a week
each. Jobshares are commonly offered in progressive local
authorities, although the take-up has always been low, and they
are slowly spreading to the private sector. Jobshares tend to be
done in junior positions in commercial companies, but they are
gradually creeping higher up the scale.

All the jobsharers who spoke to me point out that their
employers benefit because they do more than one job between
them – the employer is often getting one and a half jobs for the
price of one salary.

TERM-TIME WORKING

This allows women with children at school to work during school

---

*Birmingham City Council has usefully listed the benefits to
employers of jobsharing:*

- there is a lower turnover of staff
- there is additional cover in peak periods
- there is greater flexibility
- there is better continuity, due to less absence for domestic reasons
  and halving the impact of absence for sickness
- employees work with more energy (important in complex or
  tedious jobs)
- there are a wider range of skills, sharers can contribute different
  skills
- there is a wider employment pool which includes those who cannot
  work full-time
- jobsharers' outside interests may bring new approaches and
  knowledge to the job
- it is a way of easing people into full retirement
- the skills of those not able to work full-time are retained.

hours during term-time. Boots, for example, has a term-time working contract and some local authorities, like Oxfordshire, also have this arrangement and other similar schemes to allow flexible working.

WORKING FROM HOME

Many of the hi-tech companies, such as International Computers Ltd (ICL), will fit computers in their employees' homes. ICL started CPS, which is their teleworking unit, as they call working from home, in 1969. The company now employs hundreds of women on flexible hours contracts, many of them returning to full-time work on site after a few years. A manager in Planning at Shell works three days at home and two in the office, because it takes so long for her to get to work and back that she would not see her daughter if she travelled to and from the office five days a week.

WORKPLACE NURSERIES

The talk these days is all of workplace nurseries, but they are few and far between. The Working for Children Campaign says that workplace nurseries provide reliable childcare. They help reduce the anxiety of parents, they have high standards, they benefit children and their doors are open to mothers who can continue to breastfeed babies without too much disruption. All the women interviewed for this book who had children in workplace nurseries found them a boon. Belinda Coote at Oxfam and Elaine Barnes from Oxfordshire County Council say that their respective nurseries are one of the main reasons for staying on at their place of work.

An Equal Opportunities Commission study by Bronwen Cohen and Karen Clarke said: 'The availability of childcare provision does not determine the number of mothers in paid employment but the type of childcare provision available determines the sorts of jobs women can do in terms of hours, location, etc.'

However, workplace nurseries are not always the answer. They are
not suitable for women who work long or erratic hours, nor often
for parents who live a long way from their work, and they are
redundant once a child goes to school. Every working parent of
a school-age child knows just how many hours there are still left
to cover.

The Save The Children Fund have further reservations about
workplace nurseries: they can disrupt children who are brought
up away from their neighbours and their future schoolfriends.
Kate Harper, the main union representative at the charity, told me
that when they questioned parents working for the charity about
what childcare arrangements suited *them,* they replied childcare
near home; when, however, parents were asked what the charity
should provide they responded: a workplace nursery. Kate Harper
said, 'That's because the media talks about it all the time.'

Some companies, like Research & Development Services, are
moving to buy places in nurseries near to the child's home. This
is fine if one can be found. In the UK, we lack good nursery
provision, although more workplace nurseries have been opened
in the last two years than in the preceding decade and quite a few
large companies have explored the feasibility of introducing
workplace nurseries. The Midland Bank, for example, grabbed the
headlines with the promise of 300 nurseries in four years, but
Thames Television, London Weekend Television and the trade
union, NALGO, had places in nurseries long before they were
fashionable.

Childcare: The Management Issue of the 1990s *prepared by the
Survey and Information Analysis Unit of Sheffield City
Polytechnic for Bradford Metropolitan Council in 1989:*

*The project considered the effects that nursery provision has
in helping to retain and attract staff. The underlying aim was
to estimate the cost savings to Bradford Council of its
workplace nursery.*

*The survey showed that if the nursery were to be closed 42
per cent of the parents would be likely to give up work with the
council – a conservative estimate of this cost would be £140,000.*

Some organisations pay money towards an employee's childcare expenses as an alternative to providing a nursery place. This can be a flat rate payment or it can vary according to the employee's salary or household income. Cambridge City Council, for instance, pays 75 per cent of the cost up to £40 a week. Thames Television pays low income employees a proportion of their costs.

Some groups of employees have set up welfare funds, particularly in publishing companies, which provide childcare assistance. At Penguin Books, for instance, the fund is administered by the three unions, SOGAT, MSF and the NUJ.

One problem is what to do with children over five during the school holidays. Some workplace nurseries run holiday playschemes, for instance the BBC, some parts of the Civil Service and Refuge Assurance.

These then are some of the policies adopted by companies to attract women and keep them. But do we know if these policies work in practice? This, of course, is the nub, and it is why monitoring staff in terms of how many women are being recruited and where they are on the ladder is an essential activity.

PROMOTION

In most of the companies I surveyed for this book less than 10 per cent of senior management were women and the vast majority had only one or two women on the board – and these are the good companies, the ones which are trying to change the status of women.

Of course, promotion is not just about women getting into senior management, it is about women reaching a level where they feel they are fulfilling their potential. The lack of women in senior management indicates that this is not happening. The other obvious example is how little career development is offered to secretaries. The ones who do move on tend to have bosses who encourage them to go for better positions, like Pek Har Tan at Littlewoods, who is now training to be a Personnel Officer.

So, why aren't women being promoted? If there were an easy answer to this one, the best companies would have solved the problem rather than still being in the process of tackling it and trying to break down barriers to promotion. In many companies that mythical glass ceiling that women cannot break through still exists: after a certain level within the company it is men only.

Many women interviewed in this book have spoken about the need for 'a critical mass' of women in management, so they are no longer tokens or showing the flag. Many believe that once there are substantial numbers of women in management, particularly senior management, it will become much easier for those coming up behind because it will be as 'normal' for a woman to be promoted as for a man. At the moment, promoting senior women is seen as slightly risky by the powers that be: if that woman fails her failure reflects on all women, rather than, as it is with men, only on that individual.

Once women get into management in a critical mass they might also change management. The confectionery firm Mars believes having men greatly outnumbering women in management produces a rather aggressive style whereas a higher proportion of women would allow a more caring management style to emerge, in both women and men. The feeling is that the influence of women would make management more effective and more likely to come to the right decisions because there would be more divergent points of view and backgrounds.

Many senior men, and women, throw up their hands in exasperation because they say 'women are their own worst enemy – they won't even apply for jobs'. Sometimes this is a problem of confidence; often it is a well thought-out, deliberate decision because the sacrifices are not worth it. In this country, most companies are still run by men with wives who do not go out to work but deal with the domestic chores and the children and are often also social secretaries and professional hostesses for their husbands. Even the few women interviewed in this book who have husbands who have given up paid work to look after the children, expected to share the care and responsibility for their children. Few mothers want a job which entails being, at best, a weekend parent. Those women who are not mothers still want a life outside work: often when they look at the life styles of the male senior managers they do not see an image of what they would like to be.

The women in this book talk about the praise managers receive not for the work they achieve but for the hours they put in at their place of work. The time has come for British companies to question the hours management are expected to work. How fresh and efficient can one be working a sixty to eighty hour week?

The barriers to women's promotion are complex and they cannot be attributed just to the time lost or opportunities missed due to the demands of having children. Women without children do not abound in senior management. Perhaps women lack the support of mentors, those senior people who encourage and speak up for their protégés. Most of the successful women in this book were encouraged by senior men. It is tempting to wonder how many women were not given this opportunity. Where are they now?

Another barrier to promotion could be the way women are assessed throughout their career: they are often given annual appraisals by senior men. Roger Bennet writing in *Women in Management Review* on 'How Performance Appraisals Hurt Women Managers' says, 'the simple fact [is] that the overwhelming majority of existing senior managers, who appraise the performances of subordinate female staff, are men. And they evaluate the performances of female juniors from essentially masculine points of view ... Appraisal processes should be vehicles for coaching and developing female employees, with managements accountable to their female subordinates for the training and planned experience they need to progress. Companies offering guaranteed promotion will undoubtedly attract the highest calibre of female management trainee.'

It is often a change of attitude, of perception – an ability to think along new lines – that is needed to see the potential of women managers. Victoria Hillier, a British Telecom manager, won a company scholarship to study women in engineering management for four months. The first unnecessary barrier she discovered was 'a belief that to be an engineering manager one has to be an engineer. But looking at what the job is – human resource management responsibility - one only needs an appreciation of the technical; a training course is enough for that. This opens the door for non-science graduates and women working up the company from areas like sales.'

Progressive companies say that they do not allow maternity to block the women they value. A number of women in the book were promoted while on maternity leave: Fiona Chesterton of the BBC is one such example, she was made Editor of the South-east of England's regional news programme; Leonie Lonton of Save The Children Fund is another. Ms Lonton was promoted to Overseas Personnel Manager with a young child and cut the travelling down to two trips a year abroad, each of two weeks. She is still able to do the job as efficiently and she saves the charity money.

To what extent then are companies following Roger Bennet's advice and equipping women for promotion with enlightened and good training policies?

TRAINING

The best companies provide training for their staff at all levels, throughout their career, so employees are always encouraged to realise their potential. Sometimes women do not recognise the

---

A study which is still in progress, entitled Higher Education and the Labour Market *(HELM), is following a sample of 1982 graduates and shows how women graduates underachieve in the labour market in comparison with men. They earn less, have lower status jobs and more limited promotion prospects:*

- After three years 40 per cent of the men and 17 per cent of the women were in higher grade management or the professions
- 83 per cent of the men and 93 per cent of the women were earning less than £7,000 after one year
- 21 per cent of the men and 38 per cent of the women were earning less than £7,000 after three years
- After three years 35 per cent of the men and 19 per cent of the women were earning more than £10,000.

skills they have and lack of confidence in their own qualities can stand in the way of advancement. Many companies have arranged women-only courses to combat this. Rank Xerox and the Rover Group both run assertiveness courses which also cover career-planning. British Telecom runs monthly seminars on assertive management for women. Following pressure from the union because of the number of women in low-grade employment, ICL allowed every woman in the company to go on a training course within an eighteen-month period. The Midland Bank has a year-long degree course for clerical staff to increase the number of women managers. Esso sponsored thirty-three women on an Esso Management Course for women run by the Pepperell Unit of the Industrial Society; some of them were women from the company but others were from teaching, banking and engineering.

Any woman applying for any job at any age would do well to discover what their potential employer has to offer in terms of training, and indeed whether training is available for all staff at each and every level of that company. Another question to ask is whether that company sets targets.

TARGETING

Targeting for promotion is not a quota system, but a way of seeing if the equal opportunities policies are working: if the targets are not being met there are still blocks to women in the system which need to be sorted out. Mars has set targets for getting women into management, so have the BBC, London Weekend Television and the British Council. Leicester City Council has targets for different departments which are broken down into management and non-management.

> *In 1986, the Chair of the Manpower Services Commission, Bryan Nicholson, said, 'If the process of promotion and development were working properly, about 44 per cent of senior management would be women.'*
>
> *By 1988, 15 per cent of all management or management related posts were held by women, which was a 5 per cent increase over ten years.*

This is all well and good, but targets can only be used
successfully in combination with training and support or a woman
can be left isolated in a job she is not sure she is capable of. Many
women are worried about targets and quotas, particularly in male-
dominated areas, where the men can object to what they see as
favouritism. However, targeting is encouraging women with
ability to achieve their potential and redressing the constant
discrimination, however unconscious, that has always militated
against them at work, rather than promoting incompetents just
because they are female. To make targets work there has to be a
change of attitude throughout the company, an understanding of
why an equal opportunities policy is needed. Far too many women
told me that while the company as a whole has very good policies,
some individual male managers find successful women
threatening and do not tend to promote or encourage them. This
is a problem which cannot be blamed on individual companies;
sadly, it is a widespread problem in our society, which is bad for
both men and women. Nevertheless, women are forever being
exhorted to be more assertive, gain more confidence, not to find
powerful men daunting and generally go for it, and then we have
to pussyfoot around the fragile egos of powerful men because they
find us threatening. This makes me angry but I hope that *Best
Companies for Women* shows readers that it can be done, that
women are making inroads and changing companies' and
individuals' assumptions about what their merits are.

The Report of the Hansard Society Commission on *Women at
the Top* of course found very few women at the top. However, it
did conclude on an optimistic note:

> 'There are still formidable barriers which stop women getting to
> the top: of structures, of working practices, of tradition and above
> all, of attitude. But there is strong evidence of what organisations
> can do to break down all these barriers. It would take only a small
> amount of determination to make sure this country ceases to under-
> use nearly half its talent. We urge Government and Parliament,
> industry and commerce, the professions, academia and the various
> branches of the public service to act on our recommendations, so
> that we may cover at speed the last long mile of the journey towards
> equality. It can be done.'

WHAT MAKES A COMPANY GOOD FOR WOMEN?

A good company for women is one which does its best for its employees, encouraging potential to be used most effectively and taking into account individual needs and demands. The particular skills and qualities of an employee are valued, instead of trying to make that person live up to a stereotyped 'company man' image.

The best companies for women are also, of course, the best companies for men.

USING PART 2

Part 2 of this book details the fifty companies I have chosen as the best. Each entry begins with a brief description of the company and who it employs. This is followed by a chart so that the reader can see at a glance which equal opportunities policies the company operates, such as part-time working or a sexual harassment code. Then the bulk of the entry describes how the company works in practice and what it is like to work there according the the women I interviewed.

The Honourable Mentions are those companies which have not made the top fifty but have started taking women seriously. The lists at the back of the book detail policies and which companies have adopted them. If you are interested in a certain policy you should consult the relevant list.

PART 2

The 50 Best Companies

COUNCILS

*Cambridge City Council is Labour controlled. It is the
planning authority for Cambridge and provides local
authority housing; leisure services – from parks to pools,
cemeteries to the Cambridge Folk Festival; refuse collection
and street cleaning; environmental health and protection –
from dog wardens to meat inspectors; highway maintenance;
and, of course, the poll tax. The council employs 1,316 people,
almost half of whom are women.*

Cambridge City Council

Equal Opps Policy	✓	Crèche	✗
Equal Opps Recruitment	✓	Career Breaks	✓
Monitoring	✓	Jobshares	✓
Positive Action	✗	Flexible Hours	✓

Jan Hare, the Principal Policy Officer for Cambridge City Council
is quite lyrical about what has happened to the council: 'Two to
three years ago the winds of change whisked across the country
and even blew in here.' Those winds might have left much
unsettled, with policy and practice not always matching each
other, but they have transformed the position of women,
particularly mothers.

Megan Collyer is a Business Planning Adviser dealing with the
use of computers. She has built up her skills whilst having three
children and moving around the country to follow her husband's
job. The council was grateful for those skills and willingly
employed her on a part-time basis eighteen months ago. Within
six weeks, she was project leader, and now has a special contract

giving her an extra ten days holiday a year, with a four-day week during the summer holidays.

While Ms Collyer thinks the council is 'a bloody odd organisation', she says it is good for women: 'A lot of the perks are in the main for the benefit of women, like the childcare subsidy which used to be for the under fives and is now for up to 14 years. There is part-time work and jobsharing. Four of the Chief Officers are women, and two of those have children, so they're understanding about crises. If you're prepared to do a good job and work hard the minutes don't count.'

Ms Hare has also worked for other councils 'where it really is sleepy hollow', and says Cambridge is more of a partnership between council members and council officers.

Nicky Glegg, a Housing Information Officer, came from the voluntary sector 'where almost all the staff are women – much of it run by dynamic women'. She finds working in a department where all the senior people in the top two tiers are men 'an irritation'.

Ms Glegg is a jobshare but says she has chosen this because she can afford to have time for herself, rather than needing to meet the demands of being a single parent to 11-year-old Polly. However, it did allow her time to help settle Polly into secondary school, and makes it possible to care for her after school. She found going into a jobshare a terrible shock and took months to organise her time. She also felt there was some antagonism from her colleagues: 'Part-time for children is sacrosanct, but there is suspicion about taking it for yourself. There is little respect for that space.' However, she says, 'it's brilliant'.

She commends the council on its childcare policy, which includes a holiday playscheme for staff children and plans for a workplace nursery: 'It's exceptionally good and makes it easy for parents. It is institutionalising flexible working, such as term-time only and other part-time arrangements.' The council also has several people working part of their week from home.

Ms Glegg's main complaint about the council is that the authority is inconsistent. Policy is dependent on the whims of particular departments and is not communicated to employees effectively. Ms Glegg noted: 'I only found out recently that the council allows up to five days compassionate leave for looking after children and I am the Equal Opportunities Rep.'

Jan Hare says the council is still a male-oriented organisation: 'Whilst I don't feel I have suffered and don't tend to get het up, there clearly are some women still hemmed in and held back. There is still a culture change to go through. There is resentment in some quarters about the number of things the council does for women. There are still many changes needed – people feel threatened and uncertain.

'I would say we are very good on policy but the practice leaves a little to be desired. For instance, there is a corporate strategy about valuing the staff and then they close the canteen and talk about taking away free car-parking places.'

Whatever her reservations, Ms Hare enjoys her work: 'I really love my job and like working for the City Council. I am a fairly political animal and it is a politically charged place. There is a lot going on and it keeps you on your toes.'

Megan Collyer describes her job as a 'constant hassle', but adds, 'I thrive on hassle.' There have been two occasions when she has almost walked out, but as she was responsible for implementing the poll tax system in Cambridge one can understand her saying it was a difficult time: 'I must quite like it or I wouldn't still be here.'

Jan Hare commends the council on its commitment to training staff: 'If you want to go on a course, you put your name down and go. I went on a three-day management effectiveness course for women and got a tremendous amount out of it. I found it exactly what I wanted. I needed to have confidence that I did have useful skills.'

In a university town with light and hi-tech industry needing skilled workers, the council has found a way to compete effectively and to begin implementing a genuine equal opportunities programme for women.

Nicky Glegg sums the current position up: 'I think we're very lucky in that we have a lot on paper, although we have enormous attitude changes to make. There are still not enough women senior managers, but people are talking about it. Nine-tenths of the problem is raising it. Women are progressing through the

organisation, and now they are moving much quicker. It is just
uneven. We are talking about co-operation and it will happen.'

As the staff of Cambridge City Council know, equal
opportunities is much more than just instituting good policy. The
council seems set on the more difficult task of shifting attitudes.

Edinburgh District Council is Labour controlled. It deals with all the housing, recreation and cleansing for the city. Almost 40 per cent of the 5,000 employees are women: half are manual workers, mainly cleaners and catering staff, the other half are white collar, ranging from clerical workers to those in senior management positions.

Edinburgh District Council

Equal Opps Policy	✓	Crèche	✓
Equal Opps Recruitment	✓	Career Breaks	✗
Monitoring	✓	Jobshares	✓
Positive Action	✓	Flexible Hours	✓

Edinburgh District Council is thought by some of its women employees to be one of the best employers in Scotland. Certainly it combines a commitment to training and promotion of women with provision of flexible working and a crèche.

It was the subsidised nursery that wooed Denise Fraser back after the birth of 18-month-old Stephanie: 'It's ideal, absolutely ideal. I don't think that I would have come back if it hadn't been available.'

This was the first local authority workplace nursery in Scotland, and for many women who now use it, its very existence sums up the commitment the council has shown to encouraging mothers back to work.

Ms Fraser could have requested to come back part-time or she could have jobshared if she had chosen to, because the council tries to adapt to mothers' needs when they return to work. She is a Personal Assistant to the Director of Technical Services and says that what she needs is training: 'In my position, it is the only hope of moving on. I tend to be overlooked for advancement. I need day-release courses.'

The council is promoting more training for women. Violet Iwanio joined the Department of Personnel and Management Services in 1988 as a professional trainee and attends college once a week to study for the Institute of Personnel Management qualification: 'As a trainee, I attended several relevant internal training courses. The training programme itself provided me with the opportunity to gain the appropriate experience and abilities which enabled me to apply for promotion. In March 1990 I was appointed to the post of Professional Assistant in the staffing section. The council encourages its employees to go on training and further education courses which are relevant to the job.'

Ms Iwanio is a single parent but has found that this is no drawback: 'I myself raised it at the interview, but only to explain why I had been out of the workplace for the previous two years. In work it just doesn't count at all.'

There are women-only courses:

▌ Assertiveness for Women (held twice a year)

▌ Job seeking skills for women (held once a year)

▌ Management techniques for women (held once a year).

According to Ms Iwanio there are a number of women in middle management positions, up to Assistant Principal, but above that women are few and far between. The council has a positive action programme which encourages women to seek promotion, but out of the fifty-five senior people at Director, Assistant Director and Deputy Director level, only four are women, so there is a lot of work to be done.

One of those women is Leslie Evans, the Assistant Director of Recreation with special responsibility for the arts. She has not worked her way up but gained experience in other councils and in working for arts organisations. She came in as Senior Arts Officer, left to work for Stirling District Council for eighteen months, and then returned to Edinburgh District Council as Assistant Director. She loves her job: 'There aren't many other jobs in Scotland in the arts which would be as appealing or pay as well. It's one of the most senior jobs I could do in Scotland and I will be perfectly happy here for at least the next two or three years.'

She has more mixed feelings about the council: 'It is frustrating, because it is more bureaucratic than other councils I have worked for. Edinburgh takes a positive view towards innovative ways of working and is prepared to consider new approaches, but can take a long time to put them into practice.

'For racism or sexism, there is quite an education process to go through; there is innate sexism here which is irritating, but this is the case in most organisations.

'However, things are changing. The people who appointed me don't have a blinkered approach. The Recreation Department is excellent and the Director is very good, which makes a massive difference. He is very aware of the whole women's issue and makes a genuine effort to implement the policies, helped by two women in senior management and the Women's Unit.

'Sex certainly isn't keeping me back, partly because I haven't allowed it to, but also because I have had supportive superiors, always men, who have encouraged me to go further than I would have thought myself capable of.'

Ms Evans has recently married and would possibly like children in the future, but: 'It would be impossible to manage this job as I do currently with a child. I go out up to five nights a week. The idea of combining this career with children is daunting, but I will do it.'

Whatever her slight frustrations might be, she feels quite lucky: 'There is no question that Edinburgh Council is probably more supportive and understanding than most employers in Scotland.'

Gloucestershire County Council is in the heart of the Cotswolds and Forest of Dean areas. It is currently a hung council, with the Liberal Democrats as the largest and hence controlling group. Gloucestershire, like all County Councils, runs education in the 400 or so schools and four Further Education Colleges; is in charge of social services, including day centres and residential homes; builds and maintains the roads; provides library services across the county; and runs the fire service. Its slogan is 'At Your Service' which says much about the new spirit of customer care that has developed across County Councils like Gloucestershire in recent years. It has about 17,000 employees; some 13,000 of them women.

Gloucestershire County Council

Equal Opps Policy	✓	Crèche	✓
Equal Opps Recruitment	✓	Career Breaks	✓
Monitoring	✓	Jobshares	✓
Positive Action	✓	Flexible Hours	✓

In the summer of 1986 Gloucestershire decided to take on equal opportunities, for gender, disability and race. There was nothing piecemeal about its approach: a strategy was worked out dealing with recruitment, promotion and the special needs of all three groups. Much of the impetus was led by the then Chief Executive, Michael Bichard, who has since left, Mohan Yogendran, who is now Recruitment and Equal Opportunities Officer, and a committed group of councillors who spanned the political groups.

The rationale in 1988, when the 'Working For Equality Plan' was first implemented, combined the need to ease recruitment problems by taking on those groups traditionally passed over, and to keep on women who tended to leave after having children. It also aims to provide better services to the community by ensuring that the council workforce reflects and represents the different

types of people in the community. It sets actions and targets for
every department on an annual basis and measures their
performance against these actions and targets.

Barbara Webster, Senior Assistant to the Chief Executive, came
from Birmingham City Council in 1989. She is one of the most
senior women in the county council and has become involved in
its equal opportunity activities, but does not underestimate the
challenge: 'I don't think it's easy and it takes time because we are
forever consulting with people about what we do.

'At heart, it is about management changes. We are trying to
improve the position of women employed within the council and
women tend to be concentrated in certain areas and the lower paid
jobs. Every year each department has to produce an action plan
on how it is going to improve: for instance, the fire service now
has two women firefighters.'

Ms Webster is one of a small minority of women in senior posts –
only one in eight of senior managers are women compared with
71 per cent of the workforce: 'Action is being taken to improve the
representation of women in senior posts. We are helping to develop
a network of women managers supported by chief officers.' There
is a monthly day-course, Effective Career Development for
Women, which is an acknowledgement that attention has to be
paid to the specific career development needs of women. In
addition, monthly Confronting Inequality courses are run for
managers to encourage them to be aware of equal opportunities
and make use of equality initiatives to get the best out of their
staff.

Ms Webster feels that getting more senior women is not just a
matter of fairness: 'Quite a lot of women feel that women have a
different management style – the women feel the practical skills
they have to offer are not fully understood or valued. Talking to
some of the more senior women managers, they generally enjoy
working here: at one level, women are accepted, but they are not
always taken on as equals.'

To keep women on after motherhood, the council has introduced
a number of measures. A nursery for staff children opened in 1991
and a childcare allowance has been operating since 1989.

Sue Killoran, secretary to the County Library, Arts and

Museums Officer, had 5-year-old Daniel before the crèche started. There was no nursery provision for under twos in Cheltenham, where she lives, and she had to take him to a nursery in Gloucester. Now he has started school, she is allowed to start later; she drops him off on the way to work and a childminder picks him up. Ms Killoran is grateful for the £15 a week child allowance: 'The council is getting better and better. It has been recognised that many women want to return to work, but there is a lack of facilities for the under fives.' Gloucestershire has completed a review of all services for the under fives and realises that lack of childcare is a major issue.

Ms Killoran enjoys her job and has no wish for promotion, but Ms Webster says that often women like her get overlooked: 'Even among women there often is a lack of concern about secretarial staff. They are not valued and fundamentally that has not changed.'

Alison Laverick, an Educational Guidance Worker with two children, has taken up the council's jobshare scheme. She even managed to move with her jobsharer, Linda, from the Probation Service to the Education Service: 'It has worked really well. We are mates and talk outside work, so they get two brains for the price of one. I'm much more responsible working to Linda's requirements, I would never let her down.'

In the eight years she has been with the council, she has seen dramatic improvements, putting the driving force down to the former Chief Executive: 'It feels to me a damn sight better than it was. There have been a lot of changes, but attitudes and awareness have a hell of a long way to go. There is a lot going on about policy information, but it is not being channelled. There is a bit of a limbo about where the policy is going to go next and how it will be implemented. At least people are trying to embed equal opportunities in policy rather than just tacking it on.'

Ms Webster is also worried about how far the council has gone: 'Any equal opportunities organisation has to address whether expectations are right. Have we changed our attitude to how important work is in relation to family life, children and looking after the sick and elderly?'

The fact that the council is beginning to tackle these attitude and, perhaps more importantly, behavioural changes among managers as well as staff, says a lot about how far down the road of equal opportunities Gloucester has already travelled.

*Leicester City Council is a Labour controlled council which
deals with most of the public services in the city from
emptying dustbins to collecting the poll tax. The council is in
charge of council housing, environmental health and parks
and swimming pools in the city. It employs 1,570 women out
of its 4,137 employees. Within these figures 2,481 are white
collar jobs, of which women occupy 1,224.*

Leicester City Council

Equal Opps Policy	✓	Crèche	✓
Equal Opps Recruitment	✓	Career Breaks	✓
Monitoring	✓	Jobshares	✓
Positive Action	✓	Flexible Hours	✓

Leicester City Council proudly boasts that it often advises the
better known radical London councils on implementing
progressive policies for women. While the latter garner the
publicity and try to duck the flak, Leicester quietly gets on with
the job.

Kathy Reid, a Personnel Officer (Policy Development), believes
the initiatives introduced by the council since June 1983 have
become standard practice and have made the overall working
climate much better. Women are still employed mostly in white
collar jobs and only forty-eight of 292 management posts
(Principal Officer grade) are held by women. Although 200 of the
292 jobs are technical or professional posts in engineering,
surveying, planning, valuation, technical housing services,
accountancy and grounds maintenance, where women are very
poorly represented nationally.

The council is doing much to remedy these rather depressing
figures. There is special equal opportunities training for
recruitment, with all shortlists being monitored to try to stop
prejudice from creeping in. Every department has to produce a

'positive action programme' to improve the position of women in employment in every department; employment patterns, as well as departures and recruitment, are monitored in each department and each department has set targets, but not quotas, for the recruitment of women.

The City Council is justly proud of the amount it spends on training its staff to obtain better qualifications by sponsoring both day-release and full-time schemes. In the legal department, one woman has been given a year off, with her fees paid, to attend the local polytechnic for her law training. The council even helped her fight to get a place because she is not a graduate.

Leicester certainly appears committed to bringing out the best in their employees – particularly women and ethnic minorities. There are training schemes which are specially designed for women, and there is a particular push for Afro-Caribbean and Asian women.

Kathy Reid says the council's reputation for training means that it continues to receive large numbers of applications for its clerical and administrative vacancies. The council's pay rates for clerical posts are also a factor: the Low Pay Supplement ensures a minimum weekly wage of £154. However, the council suffers from shortages of applicants for many of the professional posts that occur nationally. Retaining staff is harder because too many people trained by the council seek the greater financial rewards and perks available in the private sector.

Mothers are more likely to stay because of the efforts the council makes to accommodate them, including a nursery, career breaks and homeworking, which is now being piloted. Ms Reid herself was offered a considerable salary rise elsewhere after the birth of her first baby but she decided the council would be a more understanding employer. She says it is a relief to have the opportunity to take a day off with compassionate leave when her child is sick so that he can either be nursed or longer-term arrangements for his care can be made.

Another attraction for mothers is that almost every job in the council is open to jobsharing. Judith Szymanski, a Planner, says it was the offer of a jobshare that made her join the Planning Department when she decided to return to paid work after having a family – a bonus for the council as local authority planners are notoriously hard to recruit: 'I was not aware of jobsharing round here, I thought it only happened in London. I wanted to work part-time and sent my c.v. to many planning departments and the council offered a jobshare. It means I can do properly paid part-time work using my qualifications.'

Sue Lockwood, Head of Legal Services, is the most senior woman in the council. She started there straight from Law School and has worked her way up. Sue has two children, she says: 'I am continuing to achieve what I want for my career without being forced to sacrifice something very personal; I have not had to choose between career and family.'

She adds: 'Things have happened since I began my articles ten years ago, when I was a rare object. Now there is an expectation that something can be worked out for women.'

In spite of the council's policy on jobsharing, she feels it was never an option at her level: 'There's a degree of realism in what I haven't asked for; I do not believe my job could be jobshared, done part-time or have fixed regular hours. I've been fortunate in continuing my career, but it hasn't been easy.'

For her the nursery, 'like the Ritz for kids', is not an option either. It closes at 5.30 p.m. and evening meetings and office crises mean she could not do her job without employing a nanny. However, she does take advantage of the childcare allowance for added expenses incurred by going to evening meetings.

The nursery takes babies over six months and has a waiting list of over a year. The workers try to be flexible for parents whose alternative childcare arrangements break down and need an emergency stopgap.

Val McCarthy, Head of the Women's Unit, worries about the depth of the commitment to women in the council, and how quickly it could be eroded in the face of cuts in services. When budgets are pruned equal opportunities could appear optional, or have less political priority in the eyes of the councillors. Ms McCarthy's greatest pride is the sexual and racial harassment policy-making: the council is the only employer in the country with a complaints officer. But she says: 'Policies are all very well but if there comes an indication they don't have to be carried out then they're worthless. If a department head doesn't like jobsharing and he makes it known, women will no longer ask for jobshares in that department, and other managers could follow suit. Equal opportunities are never safe enough to feel we have won.'

Leicester City Council is probably one of the best employers in the UK. A political commitment to equal opportunities has motivated many of the initiatives, but they have also proved to be good business sense, enabling the council to recruit better staff and retain them.

Islington Council, in north London, is Labour controlled. As an Inner London Borough Council it is responsible for housing, social services, environmental services, recreation and education. Its staff doubled in April 1990 when the abolition of the Inner London Education Authority led to the transfer of education to the boroughs. It currently employs 12,000 people, almost half of whom are women. Over the past decade the council has pioneered policies of equal opportunity and decentralisation.

London Borough of Islington

Equal Opps Policy	✓	Crèche	✓
Equal Opps Recruitment	✓	Career Breaks	✓
Monitoring	✓	Jobshares	✓
Positive Action	✓	Flexible Hours	✓

Islington Council faces a delicate juggling act: while facing continuing government cuts, it attempts both to keep up its services to residents of the borough and to offer its staff a good deal. It is a 'high spending council' which has been both rate capped and poll tax capped but nevertheless needs to attract high-quality staff. There is also a genuine commitment to equal opportunities by the council, based on political principles as well as sound management practice.

There is no qualifying period for maternity leave, so a woman can join the council when she is pregnant and still have her full maternity entitlement, which is fifty-one weeks with the first forty paid. However, if the mother does not return for at least three months, she must repay the money that is over and above the statutory minimum. On return, every effort is made to accommodate part-time work if necessary, particularly through jobsharing, although this is not guaranteed.

It was Islington's reputation for efficiency and for getting on

with the job rather than allowing its policies to languish in
committees which attracted Liz Bisset, who had two children, to
join as a jobshare Policy Development Officer. Islington's childcare
policies were an added bonus. She had worked in the voluntary
sector which she found so stretched in terms of staff and resources
that pregnancies and consequently not being able to work long
hours because of the ensuing childcare demands were seen as a
problem by the organisation. She joined another local authority,
but found herself caught up in the bureaucracy of everything
taking months to get through committees before any action could
be taken, which was equally stressful: 'I did not go to Islington
because of the staff code and policies, but the lack of them was
why I left the voluntary sector. There is something about the
working environment in Islington – it is a disciplined borough. I
feel the people I work with are serious about the work they do.
A lot of the work is thoughtful and thought out.'

She was promoted to Group Leader, following a competitive
interview, and went full-time. Then she became pregnant with her
third child: 'I discovered I was pregnant at the time I got the
promotion and it was dealt with very well. In local authorities
these things have been thought through and there is an attitude
of "It happens. That's life."'

Ms Bisset says Islington's policies are particularly good. There
is provision for taking up to three weeks off if a child is sick. She
says she rarely takes time off for ill children because, like many
senior and better paid women: 'I am more likely to have
supporting structures, such as paid childcare, but if one of them
did become very ill that provision would be there for me to use.
It is part of a supporting structure which Islington has, so if there
are catastrophes the strains are lessened.'

The council's child sick leave policy is open to abuse, but Ms
Bisset says: 'There is no evidence that child sick leave is an area
of widespread abuse – it is there to be used if it is needed. The
expectation of those opposed to it, that it would be widely
exploited, have not been borne out.'

Ms Bisset believes that the benefits package does attract
women, particularly into skilled areas where recruitment is
difficult because there are shortages of skilled people throughout

the UK, but the package is often omitted when advertising for staff: 'Recruitment and retention packages emphasise what is good for men, like cars, whereas many of those benefits which are particularly attractive to women tend to be ignored, like professional training packages. It is not just the overt material benefits but other things in the package which people take into account.'

Mothers in the council are still guilty about the demands of their children. Liz Bisset says: 'I'm one of the latest into the office, I come in at 9.30 a.m. because I drop the children off at school. A lot of people don't have children and come in earlier, so I do feel slightly stressed coming in later.'

There is a nursery for staff. Because it would be so massively oversubscribed there are strict criteria for places, with single parents on low incomes at the top of the list. For those on low wages it is heavily subsidised, with fees ranging from £5 to £37.50 a week. A second nursery is opening aimed at teachers and other hard-to-fill posts in the council, and charges will be up to £60 a week.

Sally Brooks, who is 37 and a Project Manager in the Architects Department, has an 11-year-old daughter, Molly. Her only criticism of the policy is that there is no flexi-time, so her hours are pre-scheduled and can not be adapted to the needs of her daughter. Like many of her colleagues, she was a late entrant into architecture. While the department is male dominated, 'more and more women are coming in and we are moving up slowly. We are getting promoted from the lower grades up, we just started later.'

Wendy Thomson, an Assistant Chief Executive in her late thirties, has been with the council for four years and says she is typical of many of the senior women in the council in that she did not come through the ranks but entered with professional qualifications and experience. She acknowledges that there are tensions between an open recruitment policy, which Islington relies on, and internal promotion. Internal promotion may sometimes be a matter of seniority but it can help women climb the ladder.

Nevertheless, Islington prides itself on its training, helping staff to obtain the skills, confidence and qualifications to do their job.

In departments like building works and architecture, the 120 trainee posts are mostly filled by women and Black people: 'This equips them to gain access to, and climb up the technical and professional ranks,' Ms Thomson says.

Islington is a left-wing Labour council and job satisfaction comes to Wendy Thomson from sharing its aspirations: 'I wanted to work for a progressive local authority. It is interesting work because I share the social objectives. There are opportunities to do different things over a wide area and I like working in a democratic organisation.'

She believes her current job would be very difficult to combine with caring for young children: 'I work with unpaid, elected councillors, many of whom have jobs during the day. As a result, I work long hours and a lot of early mornings and evenings.' For her, it works well: 'I chose Islington, live locally, and, luckily, it also took me. It has twenty-four neighbourhood offices and I am a keen decentraliser. It is an organisation which can make and carry out decisions and there is a political coherence about what it wishes to do.'

It is that 'can do' mentality, mentioned by many staff, combined with its progressive employment policies, which make Islington Council a good place to work.

Oxfordshire County Council is one of those councils on which no political party has overall control; it has its headquarters in Oxford. It employs 17,500 people, almost 75 per cent of whom are women. The largest group of women are teachers, there are also many women in the Social Services Department and Leisure and Arts, mainly in the libraries as well as women manual workers such as cooks and cleaners.

Oxfordshire County Council

Equal Opps Policy	✓	Crèche	✓
Equal Opps Recruitment	✓	Career Breaks	✓
Monitoring	✓	Jobshares	✓
Positive Action	✓	Flexible Hours	✓

Oxfordshire County Council is competing for skills with many companies in London and the Home Counties that can offer much higher salaries. It has a bigger proportion of women than most councils – 77 per cent of the staff are female, and of these almost two-thirds work part-time. A number of packages have been devised to attract women to the council, which might not give as much money as neighbouring commercial organisations but offers training combined with flexible hours.

Juliet Nesom has been with the council for two years. Before that she had not been in paid work for ten years as a result of having two children and because of her husband's job in the RAF, which meant that they were constantly moving. She had been a shop assistant with no qualifications and she is now on the council's training scheme. She has already passed shorthand and typing and is taking a two year part-time B Tech National Diploma in Public Administration.

She says it has been wonderful: 'It couldn't be better. It has given me a totally new lease of life and changed me completely. My husband says it is like living with a different woman. I see life in a different way and definitely have more confidence.'

Training women up does not always benefit the council in the long term. Ms Nesom is not sure whether her future lies with being promoted within the council or going into the private sector.

The council also encourages women to return after maternity leave. One of the benefits is five council nurseries. Elaine Barnes, an Assistant County Careers Officer with two children in one of them, says: 'It's great. I sometimes wonder if the kids go to nursery because I'm working or I work so the kids can go to nursery. It's just one huge family there.

'It made the whole difference to me going back. It solved all the problems. The nursery opened when I was pregnant with my first one, Thomas, so I booked him in as a bump.' She was lucky, the nursery now has a fifteen-month waiting list.

Even so, Ms Barnes found full-time work too much after being back for six or seven weeks: 'I really was struggling. I got very fed up and felt I couldn't handle it. I spoke to Personnel, my own boss and someone in the Working Parents' Network. I explored the possibility of reduced hours: I am now on a seven-day working fortnight. I get every Friday off and alternate Mondays.'

This system has changed her: 'I work a lot quicker and harder and achieve almost the same. There has been no lessening of responsibilities.'

In the four years since Ms Nesom's first pregnancy, 'when the equal opportunities policy was in its infancy', she has noticed enormous changes in the council: 'Everything has expanded. We have moved light years. The policies are good but the question is, how are they implemented within each section or department? My experience has been entirely positive and I have had a very good boss, but what about everywhere else?'

Linda Hackett is the Administration and Revenue Manager who pioneered part-time work for senior managers when her son Christopher was born eight years ago: 'In those days there were no women managers who had returned to work after having children. I didn't want to come back to any old job, I wanted to come back to a career. I came back full-time but after eighteen months I wanted to spend more time at home, but also continue with my career.

'As no manager before had gone part-time, I agreed to take a parallel post which could be worked twenty-five hours a week. I felt I had to really prove myself here and made sure I had no time off work. I didn't want management to look at me as a special case.

'I was upgraded because of extra responsibility and then promoted to be a senior manager. I am now in charge of four sections, forty staff and I work twenty-seven and a half hours a week. I take my son to school and leave at 2.30 p.m. so I can pick him up. It's a happy compromise and I think my son's benefited from it.' She admits she does more than her hours, taking reports home and sometimes returning to work after her husband gets home.

The climate has changed so much since she returned from maternity leave that, in her section, staff are asked what hours they want to work when they are taken on and when they return from giving birth: 'Back in 1983 I was one of the few, but now the numbers of women coming back to work and proving they can cope means mothers have gone up in people's estimation.'

The council offers good promotion prospects for women. In the period 1986-9:

∎ 25 per cent of those appointed to senior management positions were women
∎ 70 per cent of those appointed to white collar jobs were women
∎ 60 per cent of those appointed as head teachers or equivalent were women.

Oxfordshire County Council appears to have a good equal opportunities policy which benefits both the council and the women working for it.

*Sheffield City Council is Labour controlled. It runs many of
the services in the city, including the 250 schools and six
tertiary colleges; social services, from meals on wheels to
adoption; recreation, which includes parks, sports halls,
libraries, museums and the arts; and council housing. It
employs just over 29,000 people, some 18,000 of whom are
women who range from manual workers to senior managers,
including teachers, school meals supervisors, cleaners, social
workers and nursery nurses.*

Sheffield City Council

Equal Opps Policy	✓	Crèche	✗
Equal Opps Recruitment	✓	Career Breaks	✓
Monitoring	✓	Jobshares	✓
Positive Action	✓	Flexible Hours	✓

Sheffield City Council has developed some excellent policies for
women. Putting them into practice has proved somewhat more
difficult, however they do have a female Chief Executive, Pamela
Gordon.

Marilyn Hale is definitely a success: Chief Administrator for the
Works Department, she is not only one of the 10 per cent of senior
management who are female but also heads a male-dominated
workforce with a staff of 800.

She was originally appointed as Deputy and was such an oddity
that people came in to look at her: 'Everyone assumed I was a
token appointment. I think, at least I hope, since I joined the
department they have changed their ideas. When my boss took
early retirement, I applied for his job and got it. I was well
qualified. Eight years before coming to the council, I had worked
in technical departments. I knew about the Works Department
and felt I could make a valuable contribution.

'To get things done, I feel I have to work far harder than my male contemporaries and do everything better. I have not been readily accepted by other managers. Councillors are keen on equal opportunities; they firmly believe jobs can be done by women. But the officers in departments where there is an absence of women take a long time to change cultures. They treat you as a woman instead of a professional.'

Ms Hale has put her experience to good use. In 1986, the Personnel Department called a meeting of senior women managers interested in a training programme to encourage women to become managers and be successful. Out of this meeting came a positive action initiative, a two-week course for potential women managers. Ms Hale recalls: 'It was about theory, practice and sharing experience. I also became a mentor for some of them. In terms of progression and where they are all now, they have done extremely well. Some of it is due to that course. Since then, there has been another course. I sent my deputy as mentor, who took people from my department. It followed a similar pattern.'

Ms Hale says these courses were important because 'in general women managers are excellent, but they lack confidence. They are so keen to do a good job, but they think they are failing. Given the opportunity their performance is better than the average man.'

She is a member of the Equal Opportunities Task Team, which tries to ensure equality of opportunity in all areas, is Women's Link Officer and has written a 'Women's Positive Action Report'.

Ms Hale says it is impossible to generalise across the council about how successful women have been in overcoming barriers in recruitment and promotion. The results are dependent on which line the managers one is dealing with take and there are still a lot of old-fashioned ideas about.

Yasmin Farooq is a social worker specialising in Asian families. She believes it is easy to generalise about the deal women from the ethnic minorities are getting – it is not very good: 'I don't know if they are a good employer of women – it's like anywhere else, if you are white, middle class you are more privileged.

'I haven't got any grounds for personal discrimination but I definitely feel very isolated being the only Black social worker in my division. For the first four or five years I was the only Black social worker at all. It is not easy being supervised by white men.

When I speak up for the Asian families I deal with, I am seen as their friend rather than taking my views as an objective social worker who has assessed the situation. There is no scheme to recruit more Black women and the services we offer are Eurocentric. They do not take into account the different cultures people have.

'If equal opportunities policies were implemented with all honesty it probably would improve, but I don't feel optimistic.'

Ms Farooq has benefited from the council's enthusiasm for training. She has been seconded to the Polytechnic for two years to complete a diploma in social work. However, she even finds this frustrating because she says the course is Eurocentric and offers little for her specialist position dealing with Asian families. She has no doubts that she wants to continue being a Sheffield social worker, but does not know if returning to her specialisation helps to ghettoize Black families or helps their culture to become more widely understood.

Black and Asian women have a particular struggle with the council, but it was not so long ago that white women also had little chance of advancement. Kath Stringer is the Benefits Team Leader in the Housing Department. When she started eleven years ago, she was 'at the bottom of the bottom'. There was a gender hierarchy: 'At that time for a woman to take on a supervisory role was unheard of and there were no male clerks. Then there was a dramatic change of management – many of the very senior people either retired or moved on and the people appointed in their place had a completely different view. There were better pay and conditions, and men came in on the same level. But even now, the management in the Housing Department is male dominated.'

Ms Stringer has also benefited from the maternity package. She has been doing a jobshare since Rosie was born eighteen months ago: 'It works wonderfully. It's great. I certainly do work harder – particularly on my half day. I'm paranoid about leaving things half-finished, so I work hell for leather tying up loose ends. The council get two and a half people's work out of it. We're both happy, it gives us a chance to specialise and draw on our talents, and I can watch Rosie grow up.'

The council offers a variety of options to returning mothers after they have been in full-time work, through career breaks and individual part-time arrangements which are tailored to the needs of both the mother and the council.

In these times of financial stringency for local government, many women working for Sheffield City Council are hoping that councillors will not cut back equal opportunities measures.

ENGINEERING

British Aerospace comprises four main aerospace businesses with locations in many parts of the UK: British Aerospace Military Aircraft Ltd; British Aerospace Dynamics Ltd; British Aerospace Commercial Aircraft Ltd and British Aerospace Space Systems Ltd. Other major subsidiary companies include the Rover Group, Royal Ordnance, Ballast Nedam in the Netherlands, the civil engineering contracts, and military optics specialists Steinheil Optronik in Germany. British Aerospace also owns Arlington Securities, a property development business. The company employs 127,500 people.

British Aerospace

Equal Opps Policy	✓	Crèche	✓
Equal Opps Recruitment	✓	Career Breaks	✗
Monitoring	✓	Jobshares	✗
Positive Action	✓	Flexible Hours	✓

British Aerospace is taking the problem of the few women in its workforce extremely seriously. The question is whether the message has got out from headquarters.

In 1989 a large study of all the companies in British Aerospace looked at potential barriers to women and Black people. While every company had different practices and experiences, most of the managers were white men. Both the main board of BAe and all the other company boards are all male.

British Aerospace commissioned a survey of the workforce from MORI in 1989 about attitudes to women working and the type of work they should do, which has not been released outside the company, but is being taken seriously within it. Rosemary Harper, the Resourcing Manager, says that getting any policies or initiatives taken on across the board is difficult: 'We try to act as strategic architects. We encourage directors to manage companies in a positive and proactive way, for the best practice to be developed in each company – tailored to individual needs.'

Ms Harper is in no doubt that this must entail recruiting more women and keeping them on for their whole careers: 'We want to create opportunities for women in all areas, from young women apprentices in craft and manual to graduates and postgraduates. We have strong policies for attracting women school leavers. Our companies are encouraged to develop policies for contact with schools and use women role models to bring in successful women engineers.'

Rebecca Elliott, the Head of Bidding at British Aerospace Dynamics Ltd, puts that policy into practice by going into the schools. She is the most senior woman in Dynamics and is keen to encourage more females to join her. In the sixteen years since she started, there has been only a slight improvement in the proportion of women recruited. She says: 'I think it would be a good thing if there were more women. Life consists of men and women, and there are still some offices here where there are fifty men and a couple of women employees. It can't be a good thing because they don't get the breadth of view.'

Jill Derr, the Head of Systems Integration at Dynamics, says she feels as though she has always been the token woman: 'I was the token woman on the Hatfield site and I became the token female manager. The numbers haven't increased. There are plenty of senior women in personnel and the Company Secretary is female, but not in engineering. In my function there are 400 people and only two of them are female.'

Whatever might be said at head office both women are sceptical about how much effort is being made for women, particularly in terms of keeping them on after motherhood. Mrs Elliott cites the example of a woman in the 'middle levels' who is pregnant and wants to return to work, but who will need to have some flexibility and will not be available for emergency tasks. For her there is only the offer of minimum maternity leave and pay, any arrangement above that would have to be a personal one between her and her manager and consequently her chances of promotion would be limited.

Mrs Elliott says: 'I mind because she is a good example of a competent person who has been here ten or twelve years, has a lot invested in her and is very useful. Yet the pressure on her means she will probably leave. The company has no recognition of that. It will turn a blind eye to the irregularities, but will not support her.'

Ms Derr agrees that it is as difficult to keep women as to recruit them. She says this is partly because promotion is slow in engineering, which means women who have children in their late twenties have not gone far enough up the ladder to want to come back. What is more worrying is that some women have told her that they left after having returned from maternity leave because they found the pressure from male colleagues, who said they should be at home looking after the baby, too much to cope with.

Rosemary Harper's experience is very different. She was with Military Aircraft when she became pregnant, and Military Aircraft relocated from Weybridge to Lancashire during her maternity leave. She did not want to move and, until a position was sorted out for her in Head Office, she commuted regularly, being flown up and down to Lancashire. During this period her managers changed meetings from 8.30 a.m., which would have entailed an overnight stay, to 10 a.m. to enable her and other southerners to travel up on the same day, which cut down on the amount of time she was away from her child and saved the company a lot of money.

For the women who survive, there is a bright future. The senior women in Aerospace say they have not experienced discrimination. Working in contracts, Mrs Elliott discovered that to concentrate on the Middle East was going to make things difficult for her, so she focused on the USA and Europe and her career progressed. As a woman, she tends to be noticed more often.

However, as Jill Derr says, it is slightly lonely and frustrating: 'I wish I had women I could talk to and bring on. Whenever there are women, I will try to go and encourage them, but they are so few and so far behind that I am too senior now. I also wish there were others at my level I could just turn to and chat to.'

Ms Harper is optimistic. She is certain the companies will overhaul themselves, and Rover, which has a separate section in this book, is a model for the others to follow: 'The more women who are promoted and successful, the easier it is. We need lots of different role models, such as working mothers and single career women. We are putting in place influential people and making sure they have the right vision for the future.'

Like most engineering companies, British Aerospace has a long way to go, but the head office management are determined to make the journey. It is vital for the company's future that women are recruited in far greater numbers and do not leave after having children. An enormous shift in attitudes within the individual factories appears to be necessary before this can be achieved.

Brown & Root is the largest engineering consultancy and design company in the UK, designing or providing professional consultancy services in civil engineering, marine engineering, defence, aerospace, mass transit, the nuclear industry, information technology, petroleum and chemical processing, earth sciences, agriculture, water utilisation and hi-tech industries. Brown & Root is a subsidiary of an American parent company with offices throughout the UK and worldwide. It is a predominantly male company. Female employees are, in the main, currently employed in secretarial, clerical and personnel grades.

Brown & Root (UK) Ltd

Equal Opps Policy	✓	Crèche	✗
Equal Opps Recruitment	✗	Career Breaks	✗
Monitoring	✗	Jobshares	✓
Positive Action	✗	Flexible Hours	✓

The preponderance of men in the technical areas of Brown & Root combined with perennial loss of most women when they had children led the company in 1989 to consider how to attract women back to work. There was already some part-time working in existence with a programme called the Reserve Temporary Scheme, which acts as a pool of staff available to work part or full-time as and when required.

Jobsharing, term-time contracts and enhanced maternity pay have all been introduced while career break schemes, childcare vouchers and childcare facilities were considered but put on hold.

However, there is still a dearth of women in technical areas: there are twelve female engineers out of 1,500. In the first eleven years of the graduate engineering training scheme, eleven women were recruited, all of whom have subsequently left – none to have children. In 1990 three women were recruited out of a total of thirty-six.

Jackie Carpenter, who is in her early forties, is not only one of the few female engineers but is also a project manager at B & R's Eastleigh plant. She joined six years ago after an eight-year break to have children: 'I wanted to go back to a career, not a job. But I had been a mum at the school gates for a long time and had begun slightly to doubt my ability. I had a degree in mechanical engineering and had worked four years before having children, but I wondered whether I would be able to get an engineering job.

'I did one of the first woman returner courses run by Lough-borough College for women engineers: it gave us a confidence boost and updated our knowledge with some Open University courses. I decided I was definitely going to be an engineer.

'I got a six-month contract with another company which was very good. I needed to get into the swing of working but was not ready for a high-powered job. When I joined Brown & Root my immediate reaction was not to admit that I was a woman. So I didn't opt for any special arrangements. I thought originally that if I wanted to work in a man's world I had to accept the conditions: I'm not so sure of that now. Even now, though, if people make jokes about how useless women are I just try to get in first so we are all joking about how useless they are.'

She does not believe in special rules for women, yet thinks that working mothers do have a particularly difficult time, which is often not taken into account: 'Companies should allow time off, which is very rare and can always be made up for. I used to do it, but it would be better if it were formalised. I prefer to stick to the rules. It's hard enough to progress anyway when you're odd, like being a woman, let alone if you're thought to be skiving. A flexible attitude is what is needed. When we had builders in I asked if I could work at home for a few days, I was told I couldn't because the company insurance didn't cover it. That's an excuse, not a reason.'

In her six years she has seen movement: 'I think the world is changing and I think the company is making moves in the right direction. It does need to change its environment. The position used to be: here are jobs, you can take them or leave them. Now it obviously makes good business practice to improve a few things and encourage more people to apply.

'I find it difficult to know how to improve the rules to change the atmosphere. But I would like proper flexi-time - it is appropriate in a company which works on projects.'

She admits there is little pressure for equal opportunities from within because of the lack of women, 'and I don't fight for women's rights'.

Barbara Brown, Corporate Personnel Manager, certainly fights for women's rights. As a working mother she leads by example and is on a four-day week: 'I have an extraordinarily good team working for me. I work longer hours on the days I do work and often take work home. On the other hand, I take the children to school most mornings - except when I have to go to an 8 o'clock meeting - and I make sure I put them to bed two working nights a week; my husband does the other two.

'Nobody ever says anything about me not getting in on time. I'm leaning on the credibility I built up some years ago. I know I'm in a fortunate position but I feel I've earned it.'

Ms Brown says the attitude to women has changed enormously: 'In the old days it was assumed that all women were secretaries. There are now more women at all levels. It's a policy born out of desperation rather than anything else, because of the enormous shortage of skills.'

Another senior woman is Carol Blades, who is a tax specialist. She left her job at an accountancy firm because it was rare to get a tax job in industry. The job sounded very interesting and she was offered 'a good bit more money'. She too is a woman in a man's world, normally being the only woman in meetings. She does not find it a problem and feels that people certainly listen to her: 'I just get offered the sandwiches first.'

Ms Blades' only complaint is the long hours that go with the job: 'Over the past couple of months I've done 20 per cent more time than I should. I just can't do the job in less time. I do the housework at weekends and rarely go out in the evenings because I'm knackered when I go home. It does mean work impinges on my own time. I envy people I see leaving on the dot of 5 and think what I would do if I had a long evening stretching in front of me.'

It is difficult for her to be promoted in her department because it is small, but she is being encouraged to widen her scope and move into corporate tax.

Brown & Root is certainly trying hard to attract and keep women in clerical and administrative jobs, but perhaps some attention needs to be paid to their core engineering services, to recruit and retain the women of the future.

The General Electric Company is one of the largest manufacturing companies in the UK. Its subsidiary GEC Marconi manufactures a range of electronic systems for defence and civil applications. Other subsidiaries and joint ventures supply systems and equipment for transportation, power generation and telecommunication applications, as well as a comprehensive range of domestic appliances under the Hotpoint, Creda and Cannon trade names. Other products include wires and cables, lifts (Express), building controls (Satchwell) and air moving equipment (Woods of Colchester). GEC has plants throughout the UK and is one of the largest employers in Scotland where it owns Yarrow Shipbuilders on the Clyde and GEC Ferranti in Edinburgh. It employs over 100,000 people in the UK, about a fifth of whom are women.

General Electric Company plc

Equal Opps Policy	✓	Crèche	✓
Equal Opps Recruitment	✓	Career Breaks	✓
Monitoring	✓	Jobshares	✓
Positive Action	✗	Flexible Hours	✓

GEC has been hit hard by the skills shortage in the UK because its reputation depends largely on the ability of its engineers. This has led to support within GEC for government schemes like WISE (Women Into Science and Engineering), Capability in Engineering and various other programmes to encourage women into engineering. The Essex-based businesses invite forty fifth and first-year sixth form girls to spend three days of their summer holidays learning about careers in engineering and spending time with women engineers.

GEC is comprised of many different units, often operating under different names, like Ferranti in Edinburgh. While 21,000 of the 100,000 employees are women, only 5 per cent of the professional engineers are female. GEC's management style is very decentralised with few overall company policies. However, one exception is a company-wide policy on equal opportunities, with regular training seminars on the subject.

As most managers come from the ranks of engineers and scientists, the lack of women in those disciplines means that only 2 per cent of management is female.

Anne Tweddle is one of the few. She was brought up in Northern Ireland, with its high unemployment, and she wanted a job that would give her both qualifications and experience. GEC sponsored her for a Higher National Diploma course on which there were three women and fifty-three men. She began by installing telephone exchanges. After gaining experience in other aspects of engineering, she went back to college, again sponsored by the company, and obtained a Masters Degree. She is now an engineer in the systems group of GPT.

She is pleased that GEC is trying to recruit more women: 'I went into a meeting the other day with thirty people and I was the only female in the room. To me having another woman there is great. There are more and more females appearing now, but we're still outnumbered. There are more women in software than hardware, and only two in systems.'

Ms Tweddle enjoys her work and likes her fellow engineers, and feels she has not suffered from being a woman inside the company – however, some of the people she deals with externally can be more difficult: 'I have to be strong to be taken seriously. At least a quarter don't treat me as an engineer but like a secretary.'

Her first junior management job was on a site, where she was in charge of 120 men. She says the best advice she received for that was: 'Don't make the tea.' And she never did.

Rosemary Leigh is a Departmental Manager on Electro Optics in GEC's Marconi Defence Systems. She has forty people working for her, only two of whom are women, and says she has never had a problem being a woman boss: 'I thought it might be but I was wrong.'

She commends the company on its attitude: 'I am treated very well, it is only the odd individual who is against women. The company itself is making a concentrated effort to recruit more women and treat them well. The sort of people GEC attracts are those who are really interested in their job, so it's a pleasant environment to work in.'

She joined GEC six years ago, when her daughter was 8. She has made a conscious effort not to let motherhood impinge on her work because: 'That's my commitment. When I decided to take the job I gave my whole heart to it. However, I am not sure how you solve the problem of children and work – both government and companies need to do more. Being away on maternity leave is still a big negative against women.'

A career break scheme and crèches have been established within GEC Marconi, the largest group of GEC businesses, some units offer flexible hours and it has been known for women engineers to work part-time. GEC actively encourages its subsidiary businesses to pursue enlightened policies, but ultimately it is they who take the decisions. Progress is not uniform but there are bright spots.

Lynne Holt began as an engineer and is now a Personnel Manager at GPT in Coventry. As a single mother she knows the problems and sees herself very much in the role of influencing policy – 'an opportunity to get these issues on the agenda without attracting a label for myself.

'Some women do go part-time but they tend to be on contract: it depends on local needs and attitudes. The climate is changing and the need to be flexible is realised, but it's down to the quality of line management. The policy-makers are now saying: "What are we doing to recruit and keep our staff?" They know we must get women at home back working either full or part-time.'

The perennial problem of long hours for senior personnel is as endemic at GEC as elsewhere. Both Rosemary Leigh and Lynn Holt take work back with them at night so they can see their children in the evening.

Dr Leigh has a husband who is normally home by 5.30 p.m., so she knows her daughter is being looked after, but Ms Holt is finding the juggling increasingly difficult as her son Andrew grows older and needs ferrying to activities away from home: 'I have already reached one crossroads of career versus family and

I chose family. Otherwise it would have meant moving house, school, childminder, everything, and doing it alone. I just wasn't sure I could cope. As I move into jobs with increasing responsibility, I'm worried I shall have to choose again.'

Promotion in GEC seems to be mainly based on merit, with gender rarely playing a part, and those women engineers who do stay the course appear to be well treated. One director at GPT is a 28-year-old woman: Lynne Holt stresses that this woman is there because of her skills and ability, and she is excellent.

However, both recruiting women and keeping them on is a problem for GEC. This could be because the equal opportunities message is not getting through to the line managers. Women are expected to fit in and not demand any special rules. The other problem is that GEC has a reputation for meanness and the maternity pay is still only the statutory minimum of six weeks at 90 per cent pay. However, corporately the company is set on making improvements and is keen to attract women to work for it, knowing that the more women there are, the more likely attitudes will change.

Lucas Industries plc is an engineering company. Its divisions include Lucas Aerospace, one of the leading suppliers of aircraft systems and equipment in the world, and Lucas Automotive, which supplies almost every vehicle manufacturer in the UK and several in Europe. A third division, Lucas Applied Technology, is the motive force behind the application of advanced manufacturing systems throughout Lucas businesses and to other customers worldwide. The headquarters are in Solihull, West Midlands, and there are plants throughout the UK including the West Midlands, Lancashire, Wales and London, as well as Europe and the USA and many other parts of the world. It employs 36,000 people, almost a third of whom are women.

Lucas Industries plc

Equal Opps Policy	✓	Crèche	✗
Equal Opps Recruitment	✓	Career Breaks	✗
Monitoring	✓	Jobshares	✗
Positive Action	✓	Flexible Hours	✓

Like all engineering companies, Lucas has few female staff working in technical and managerial areas and has been largely unsuccessful in its attempts to recruit and keep on well-qualified and professionally-skilled women, particularly engineers. At the Chairman's request a project team of six senior women was set up, with other contributors from various areas of the company, to examine why there are so few women in management at Lucas and what can be done to change the situation. The report, which was published in March 1990, made the point that all its recommendations for good practice should be applied throughout the company.

The facts were disheartening: 2 per cent of senior managers, 3 per cent of the technical and professional grades and 19 per cent in the administrative professional group are women. The report says of women in management: 'Typically these women are in their late twenties or early thirties, unmarried and with no children. Their average service is six years and almost half of them have a formal qualification. Almost half who have a degree have studied a science or engineering discipline, but most work outside the engineering function.'

Vivien Parker is a Product Marketing Manager who came in as an electronics engineer and has been with the company for seven years. She joined as a graduate and Lucas sponsored her to do a three year Masters Degree course, which she took 'to make me more marketable'.

She says she is used to the competitive male atmosphere and even found advantages in being a woman: 'At first you are a novelty and you get remembered. But it would be nice to have a few more women around.'

She is the most senior woman in her section and was a member of the Women in Lucas project team.

Ms Parker says she has been treated well: 'To me they've been very good. Compared to most of my contemporaries, I've done as well, if not, better.' But in general she feels there is a need to improve the career progress structure. She is now on maternity leave and arrangements have been made for her to do some of her work from home, as she has requested.

Lesley Mallard, the Director of Business Development, is the most senior woman in the company and wants more women up there with her: 'It's quite lonely at times. Definitely women and men think differently. Women have to do better and be more visible. Whenever I get the chance I hire females, but it's only happened once.'

Like all too many senior women, Lesley Mallard puts her success down to luck and says the company is often tough for women: 'Senior managers are predominantly Midlands-based engineers. The company has been revamped with new blood, but the men are still not into women being senior managers. It is difficult to break into the lower management grades, hard to get visibility. There are more of us creeping in, but it's going to take a long time.'

Jane Devlin, who is an Employee Services Officer, has worked in several divisions of the company and has recently joined Lucas Aerospace. She is in her early thirties and has had two children in the last five years: 'As well as my maternity leave I had to have about twelve weeks sick leave in the early stages of both pregnancies. My managers were understanding and supportive and encouraged me to return to work both times.' Currently she is working reduced hours, and not only does she have her children and her Lucas work but she is also doing a three year Institute of Personnel Management course, supported by Lucas as part of their continued education and training philosophy for all employees.

Ms Devlin is aware that her domestic commitments may have slowed down the career progression she might otherwise have expected, but she feels that now she has completed her family she can resume a career with Lucas once more. She found that working on the Women in Lucas project team raised her hopes about progress within the company. She is particularly pushing the recommendations concerning mothers: enhanced maternity leave and pay, career breaks and flexible working hours: 'We want to encourage women to come back. There is already some flexitime, which I think will spread, but there must be a policy laid down. If it is left to discretion, it may or may not happen.'

One of the key recommendations in the report was an Equal Opportunities Manager. Ms Mallard said: 'I think we need an agent for change if we are to make serious gains. We could at least start on a temporary basis.'

Lucas has already shown how seriously the report is being taken by appointing Kate Corfield to a senior position in the company as Project Leader, Women in Lucas. She is beginning to take action in the main areas identified:

■ Overhauling recruitment and selection

■ Initiating proper career planning and development for women

■ Taking a constructive approach to flexible working arrangements

■ Introducing career breaks

■ Improving maternity pay and leave

■ Offering reduced working hours to ease women back after maternity leave

■ Offering bursaries and sponsorships to women engineering students.

Ms Corfield says: 'Lucas strives to be a world class manufacturing company. It is therefore incompatible that we should demonstrate anything less than best practice in our employment of women. There is much to be done in building on best practice and establishing further necessary innovations. Our progress will be worth watching.'

Hiring Ms Corfield to deal with equal opportunities has shown that Lucas is determined to take action on the project team's report. It is now on the brink of transforming itself into a woman-friendly company.

Ove Arup is an international partnership of designers in engineering and architectural consultancy. The headquarters are in London, but they have projects throughout the world. These projects range from low cost rural roads to major highways, from office towers to the underpinning for a medieval cathedral, from football stadia to art galleries. It employs over 3,000 staff in the UK, some 700 of whom are women.

Ove Arup

Equal Opps Policy	✓	Crèche	✗
Equal Opps Recruitment	✓	Career Breaks	✓
Monitoring	✗	Jobshares	✗
Positive Action	✗	Flexible Hours	✓

With their commitment to training and their equal opportunities policy, Ove Arup has had a good reputation among women engineers for many years. Ten to 15 per cent of the partnership's engineering intake was made up of women, but by 1989 women made up 31 per cent of total recruitment and almost a quarter of the graduate intake.

Ove Arup realised that these women needed to be encouraged to return after having children and in 1986 introduced their career break scheme which provides flexible arrangements and preserves their promotion prospects.

Deborah Lazarus is a Project Director with two children. She had been with the company for nearly ten years when she had Alexander, who is now 5, and says: 'It was fine. There was a reasonable degree of faith that I would come back.'

After her return she was instrumental in putting together a proposal for a more comprehensive maternity scheme, including career breaks. Returning to work proved to be the right decision. She was promoted and she had no doubts that she would return

again, full-time, after the birth of her second son, Oliver, now 4.
Women who have been with the company for more than five years
receive three months pay in addition to statutory maternity pay
and when they return, provided it is within the statutory period,
a one-off payment which is equivalent to one and a half months
salary to pay for childcare.

Joanna Kennedy, a Senior Engineer who has been with the
company since 1972, came back on a part-time basis after the birth
of Peter, who is now 5 years old, which she negotiated herself.
After she had David, who is now 2, she took advantage of the
career break scheme. The career break is up to three years off
after the birth of the baby and allows for part-time work as well
as extended leave. She started back by working three days a week
and now does four.

As part of the team's leadership Mrs Kennedy is flexible about
which days she works, adapting them to the needs of each
individual project. She feels she has not been held back from
interesting projects – her team has just completed a multi-million
pound construction project. However, she feels there are limits:
'If you are part-time you can take on responsibility but not as
much or in the same way as if you are full-time. It might be quite
difficult to be the project manager on a very large and demanding
job, for example, because the client could expect you to be there
all the time. It is also partly attitudes. Some people were hesitant
about me being part-time in the beginning but accept that it
works.'

She knows it is a two-way process: 'Ove Arup's a very flexible
firm and wants to keep the good people, so it is prepared to
consider the options. Now that the policy is more formalised, it
is easier for people to go on the scheme rather than asking for
special privileges, especially younger people.

'When we started looking at maternity leave, the chairman gave
his wholehearted support to the adoption of a scheme offering
enhanced benefits. I am sure the changes are paying off, that more
women engineers are staying on once they have had children. I
would hope every leader in the firm knows it and encourages
women accordingly.'

The figures back her up. In 1989, twenty-four of the forty-four women taking maternity leave returned, and all the senior women came back.

Jennifer Felgate, a Structural Engineer, has been with Arup for five years. She says the firm is particularly good because its high profile guarantees prestigious work. She was working on the refurbishment of Tobacco Dock, in London's Docklands, using timber and cast iron – materials rarely seen these days. She also testifies to the good training provided by the company. On women she has yet to be entirely convinced: 'I think they treat women very well, but they have yet to really prove themselves. It is easy to reach middle management but not the top yet.'

Mrs Lazarus and Mrs Kennedy are two of the women who will see if the company will allow women to go to the top. Deborah Lazarus, who is one of the 2 per cent of women in senior management, said: 'I think we are treated fairly. The proportion at senior level is small but increasing. One would need to watch the next five years. I don't feel that there is discrimination.'

Mrs Kennedy agrees about the importance of the next five years: 'I would be surprised if there were no women directors by then. It is still fairly early days. It is only relatively recently that women came into the profession in any numbers.'

As is the case in most companies, the long hours that senior managers are expected to work prevent women with children from being promoted quickly to those levels. Deborah Lazarus often works a ten-hour day and expects to take work home with her. Joanna Kennedy may work part-time, but she, too, expects to work in the evening when it is necessary.

However, the two women stress how pleasant it is to work for the company. Mrs Lazarus said: 'It is a very friendly environment, a good group of people. It is very well organised which means that you do not feel part of a massive conglomerate.'

Jennifer Felgate says that when it comes down to genuinely regarding women as equals Ove Arup, like every company in Britain, has a long way to go: 'When we get an incompetent woman on the board and nobody notices we shall have arrived.'

Rover Group, which used to be a nationalised company, is now owned by British Aerospace. The company manufactures cars, car-derived vans and four-wheel drive vehicles. Rover is based in a number of sites in the south of England and the West Midlands. It employs 40,000 people of whom 2,700, or about 6 per cent, are women, who work in all areas of the company, including on the shop floor.

The Rover Group

Equal Opps Policy	✓	Crèche	✓
Equal Opps Recruitment	✓	Career Breaks	✗
Monitoring	✓	Jobshares	✓
Positive Action	✓	Flexible Hours	✗

The Rover Group has an entry in this book on its own, in spite of being part of British Aerospace. This is because many of the equal opportunity initiatives developed within Rover before the takeover have stayed with the company and have not spread through the rest of British Aerospace. Rover is a classic example of how much easier it is to implement policies when they are led from the top: Sir Graham Day, Company Chairman, has had equal opportunities for both women and Black people firmly on his agenda for a long time.

The low figures at Rover are common to all engineering companies: there are no women on the all-white board; 2 per cent of senior management and only 4 per cent of management overall are female. However, in view of the fact that only 6 per cent of the company are women, the statistics are not so bad when they are seen in context. Rover has an active policy of recruiting female supervisors, which means they should also improve the figures. It is also relevant that only 5 per cent of the female graduates who applied for jobs in 1990 wanted engineering positions - where most vacancies arise.

The Rover group is actively encouraging local school leavers who are female to pursue non-traditional careers by sending women engineers into the schools to talk about how rewarding their work is. In 1989, 21 per cent of school leaver recruits were women and 14 per cent of the graduate intake were women. Kath Ditchfield, who gives talks in schools, was sponsored by Rover to study for her university degree in Production Engineering and Management. Now, at the age of 28, she is a Project Manager, part of senior management, and is full of enthusiasm for her work: 'I've no complaints. You have to make the company work for you, but I have always had support. There are opportunities and responsibility here for young people. I have moved much faster than I expected. When I first joined, the training was excellent, but I expected to leave. Now why would I want to go anywhere else? There are so many jobs I still want to do here.

'At the moment I seem to be moving very quickly. The scope is wider than I anticipated. Perhaps for my next job I will move sideways to a different area rather than go for promotion. Promotion is important but I want a wider perspective.'

Elise McConachie joined Rover as a graduate ten years ago and is now a Chief Engineer in trim and hardware, the most senior woman in the company. She is keen for Rover to recruit more women. Of the 175 people working for her, only six are women: 'I welcome more on the basis that we need the best people and if we need the best boys, we also need the best girls. Women also have a different way of looking at cars - after all women do buy cars too. I have different comments from the men. Personally, I tend to have different views on colour mixes and matching of the trim and the feel of the material. I am more interested in aesthetics.'

She has never had a problem as a woman in her supervisory role, although she thinks she is treated slightly differently: 'I never hear swearing - presumably they modify their language in front of me.'

Neither of these women has children, although Ms McConachie does intend to: 'I think you could mix work and children. In the last couple of years I have had some rapid rises and I have been putting it off, but if I had a baby I would go back to work.'

Cheryl Curtis returned to her job as Personnel Officer about six months after having Darren. She says full-time work is not a problem but her schedule is daunting. She gets up at 6 a.m., leaves the house at 7.10, drops Darren off at her mother's at 7.35 so that she is at work by 8. She should leave at 4.30 p.m. but it usually slips towards 5 and, by the time she has picked up Darren and taken him home, it is almost 6. He goes to bed at about 8 p.m., she then has dinner and gets out her work to try to catch up, and works until she goes to bed.

In her twelve years at Rover she has worked her way up from being a secretary and now, on the brink of junior management, she is determined to continue her career. She says her manager is sympathetic: 'If I have problems with Darren being sick my boss says, "Children come first. You go and sort out your son." I think they do understand that I have other commitments, but I feel that it will count against me for promotion. Managers do work overtime and I will not be able to do it to that extent.'

Rover's initiatives are not only for single women. Maternity leave is above the minimum and the qualifying period is only one year. There is a crèche at the Solihull plant and one is being developed in Swindon; a policy on career breaks has been introduced and a pilot study on jobshares is being carried out which, if successful, will be extended to cover other areas of the company. However, there is no move towards flexible or part-time working.

It is a long-hours culture although, according to Kath Ditchfield, that may be self-imposed: 'I officially finish at 4.30 p.m. but I'm always here until 6.30 and occasionally even 1 or 2 in the morning. A lot of it is me telling myself that's what the company expect. On the other hand, everybody's manager should be making sure people don't work too long, whereas that's not the case: if they see you working too long they think that's good, you're getting the job done.'

Rover does have loyalty from its employees. Ms Ditchfield says: 'I'm committed to the company and work damned hard. I'm very proud to work where I do.'

Many of the large engineering companies have realised that getting the best out of their women employees and keeping them

on after having children pays enormous dividends. Rover was one
of the trendsetters and continues to look for new initiatives.

FINANCE

The Alliance & Leicester has branches over the country, but has two main operations bases in Hove, Sussex and Oadby, outside Leicester. Almost 80 per cent of its 5,991 employees are women. The core business deals with investments and mortgage applications.

Alliance & Leicester Building Society

Equal Opps Policy	✓	Crèche	✗
Equal Opps Recruitment	✓	Career Breaks	✓
Monitoring	✗	Jobshares	✓
Positive Action	✗	Flexible Hours	✓

In 1985 the Alliance Building Society merged with the Leicester Building Society in the biggest building society merger of that time. All personnel strategies became linked to business priorities: unless they contributed to business they should not be pursued. This meant that both recruiting and keeping staff came under the microscope of management. Losing staff was costing the society money so a drive to reduce staff turnover followed. Turnover is now below 8 per cent and there are plans to reduce it still further.

The drive to keep staff has greatly benefited women because leaving to have a baby was one of the major reasons for losing staff. The society has therefore explored ways of making it easier for women to return, and has been flexible in meeting individual needs. It has also succeeded in instilling incredible loyalty in its employees; this is particularly due to the amount of investment put into staff training in both technical and personal skills, so that they feel valued.

Women make up almost four-fifths of the society's workforce, but most of them are on the bottom rungs of the ladder. One of the eighteen board members is a woman; three out of the seventy-four senior managers are women. However, the figures begin to get better when middle management is brought into the equation: 446 or 58 per cent of the 769 managers are women.

For recruitment, generally speaking, all vacancies are advertised internally, but if no suitable candidates are available, they are then advertised through the press, job centres and careers offices. Personal specifications are drawn up for each vacancy which means that candidates are selected according to consistent criteria. Qualifications are only needed when they are an essential requirement of the job. There is a programme of recruitment and selection workshops to train line managers in effective selection techniques. Ainsley Marsden, Personnel Manager, says: 'We want to make sure we can recruit from as wide a field as possible. We are targeting under-utilised groups like working mothers and believe we have broken down some major barriers with more flexible contracts and opportunities. We are also one of the leaders in offering genuinely interesting work to people thought of as too old to change careers.'

The average earnings for men in 1990 was £14,951, which was almost double the figure for women at £8,132, but that gap reflects the position of women in the lower grades of the society rather than low or unequal pay. Pay rises are on merit only, there are no cost of living increases.

Women are getting promoted and slowly rising up the hierarchy. Miss Marsden says she hopes the Personnel Department set a good example when they put her in charge of the Oadby operation. Personnel have regular contact with managers to try and dispel the myth that all managers must be male, and attend job interviews to ensure that there is no discrimination. She believes: 'We can show that there are so many women with small children who have no problems at work that it is very, very difficult for a manager with prejudices to exercise them.'

Eileen Burke is one of the success stories; she is a history graduate in her early thirties and is now a Project Leader in Systems Development, in charge of a team of fifteen people and

mainly responsible for the cash machines network: 'All my moves
came at the time I felt was right to move. I can honestly say I have
never come across any feeling that you're not right for the job
because you're a woman.' She is the only female Project Leader,
but all the men who joined at the same time as she did are on the
grade below her. She also stresses she is no workaholic: 'I've
realised the importance of leisure and taking holidays. I think it's
becoming a general trend: of course the job is important but there
are other things in life. I think having a life outside makes you
work better.'

Jill Carlisle manages two branches, Erdington and Harbourne,
and was promoted soon after she had had a baby. She had been
a Relief Manager for the five months before going on maternity
leave which had involved her travelling all around her region.
When she returned to work after the baby she felt she could not
cope with the travelling and was offered a lower-grade job with
no loss of salary. When the offer of regional relief in Liverpool
came she accepted, and after a few months applied for her own
branch. Her husband has been doing full-time childcare, but she
stresses that it was the repeated breakdown of childcare
arrangements rather than the demands of her job which led him
to suggest that young Holly should have one of her parents at
home, and volunteered to be the one. With Holly at school now,
Jill Carlisle reckons to leave work in time to pick her up at 5
o'clock; she has dinner with Holly, puts her to bed, then often
finishes her paperwork. She tries to avoid early evening meetings.

She says she has been treated well, starting as an Assistant
Cashier six years ago: 'If you want to get on you can. They've done
so much for me I wouldn't want to let them down. That sort of
behaviour keeps the commitment of the staff. They're totally
committed to their staff and I'm totally committed to them. I don't
want to look elsewhere. Most people in my office have been there
over ten years and have come back after children.'

One of the factors Ms Carlisle puts down to her success is
training: 'I took every conceivable course you can think of.' This
is something the Alliance and Leicester is justly proud of.

Secretaries, who are caught in a career rut in many
organisations, are also encouraged to widen their horizons.

Purnima Champeneri, a secretary in the Personnel Department, is going to train to become a Personnel Officer. She is unable to do so at the moment because she has a young child, with the second on the way, and current budget restrictions have meant she may not take time off work to attend college. She does not have the time in the evenings to follow the course, but she is sure that she will when the children are less exhausting. While women have succeeded in the society she points out that there are no Asian women in senior positions; she would like to be a role model to encourage others like her.

She is intending to take advantage of the full nine months maternity leave and has been offered a career break afterwards. She also has a choice of jobsharing, part-time work or, when her children start school, term-time employment. This is open to parents with children aged 5 to 14 and will allow successful applicants to take up to ten weeks unpaid leave during the school holidays. Four weeks of the annual holiday must also be taken during the school holidays.

Certainly the Alliance & Leicester have shown that training and career opportunities for women pay dividends in career loyalty. However, time will show whether women manage to seriously infiltrate senior management.

*Barclays Bank has some 2,800 branches and offices in the UK
and around 1,200 overseas offices spread through seventy
countries. It employs some 87,000 staff in the UK, and around
two-thirds are women. Barclays has set up 327 Barclays
Business Centres to help local businesses throughout the UK.
The bank also provides other services: Barclaycard; the
stockbroking division, Barclayshare; the Corporate Division
which deals with multinational organisations; the investment
bank Barclays de Zoete Webb; the International Trade
Services Department; and Barclays money market and foreign
exchange.*

Barclays Bank

Equal Opps Policy	✓	Crèche	✗
Equal Opps Recruitment	✓	Career Breaks	✓
Monitoring	✓	Jobshares	✓
Targeting	✗	Flexible Hours	✓

Barclays Bank first instituted an equal opportunities policy in
1985. The bank has an Equal Opportunities Manager who
develops new policies and, more importantly, tries to ensure that
policy is put into practice.

Barclays says the overriding principle is that each person must
be judged on merit and ability to do the job. Family commitments
must not influence a woman's career unless she expresses a wish
for them to be considered. Then they should be discussed in a
positive way and women should not be thought less committed or
ambitious if they wish to combine careers with families. In
particular, women should be encouraged to consider management.

That is the theory. In practice, men are more likely to make a
success of their career, whether they go to Barclays as graduates
or school leavers. Nicola Swan, in her early thirties, is a Senior
Executive Manager in their south-east banking division. She went

in on the Management Development Programme for graduates and noticed both a higher drop-out rate among women, and that some of them chose not to go for promotion. She is one of the most senior women in Barclays. After nine years with the bank and having had two children, she has risen faster than her contemporaries, both male and female, but puts that down to being in the right place at the right time.

Ms Swan says the bank has been extremely helpful: 'Not that it's anything they wouldn't give anyone else. I've had no special dispensation. But the family has never counted against me: in fact, I get credit for the juggling that I have to do.'

Linda Cass is a Lending Officer in a south London branch. Having given birth to her second child she is on the Barclays career break, which gives women a choice of up to two years off, unpaid, or part-time work. She chose the latter. The bank found her a jobshare and she is very happy with this: 'I wouldn't have come back full-time but I had to work for financial reasons. I do mornings and my jobshare partner comes in at 12.30 p.m. for the handover. I had to move branches but they found me a position quite close to home with hours that suit me and a job I know.'

She feels that the price of going part-time is not being eligible for promotion. She is quite happy about that because she does not believe it is practical to promote part-timers. However, Equal Opportunities Manager Chris Lyles points out that this is not company policy: 'We are going through considerable change and the view that she has taken is a traditional one. We are hoping to introduce jobsharing more widely which, in turn, will provide a vehicle for promotion in part-time work in the future.'

Fiona Adams also took the part-time option for her career break, but decided to do it for only a year:'I needed to return to work to keep my brain ticking over. I'm halfway through and I find it fulfilling. I am at junior management level and am taken seriously. Perhaps that is a bonus of being in the Personnel Department.'

Sue Field, the former Equal Opportunities Manager of Barclays, who initiated the career breaks, thinks they helped to make the organisation more attractive to female applicants: 'If the bank can show it already has a scheme in place then it is reassuring to young women who may be contemplating having children later.'

Ms Adams says that Barclays treats women well and she points particularly to the record on training: 'Women are encouraged to train and get more qualifications.' The bank encouraged her to sit and pass her Institute of Personnel Management exams, enabling her to progress from being a secretary.

Nicola Swan also stresses training: 'The bank invests a lot in every individual. We pride ourselves on our training.' Barclays believes it is essential to train all staff and there are management development courses specifically for women.

This adds impetus to the bank's policy of encouraging women to return to work: 'It makes a lot of business sense. Women who have worked for the bank have a lot invested.' Ms Swan says the bank uses her as a role model: 'Some women don't think it's possible. It's hard but it is possible.'

Ms Swan says that a lot of women are put off rising up the ladder by the philosophy that the more senior you are the more hours you have to do. This should change because 'it doesn't even work: if you work too hard you are less effective and less interesting. It's all right for short periods but not constantly. The ethos is changing among women and men. The idea of the macho man working around the clock is outdated – it belongs to the 1980s.

'I work traditional hours in the office, 8.45 a.m. to 5.45 p.m. At the moment I work the majority of evenings after the children go to bed. But I hope this is just because it's a new job and doesn't go on too long.'

She believes Barclays is sympathetic to women. Certainly the bank has attempted to overhaul its procedures to make them easier for women: from looking at recruitment to monitoring the effectiveness of their equal opportunities policy in all departments. There are no quotas but anomalies are investigated and, if necessary, discriminatory practices changed. A job evaluation scheme ensures that the relative value of the contribution made by each job is determined objectively, without regard to the sex of the person holding the job.

In recruitment, all advertisements and recruitment literature are checked to make sure that both sexes are encouraged, and job advertisements are put in magazines or newspapers that reach women.

To counter any indirect discrimination there are no age barriers in job selection, access to training or any special schemes which choose those staff who have potential for promotion to senior management. Management staff are no longer expected to make themselves available to travel round the country, but a willingness to move may make it easier to take certain jobs in other parts of the country, while specific posts include travel.

Barclays is big enough to allow for the flexibility necessary to try to meet the demands of its individual workers, and by offering career breaks and part-time work to women returning from maternity leave the bank shows that it is not just the graduate high-flyers it wants to retain.

The Halifax Building Society, established in 1853, is the
world's largest building society with assets of over £50 billion.
It not only offers the conventional savings scheme, but gives
investment advice, insurance services, personal pensions,
savings schemes, life assurance, the Halifax Visa card,
personal loans and traveller's cheques. It has its headquarters
in Halifax, Yorkshire, and has a branch network of over 740
offices and over 2,000 agencies throughout the UK. The
Halifax employs 17,000 people, two-thirds of whom are
women.

Halifax Building Society

Equal Opps Policy	✓	Crèche	✗
Equal Opps Recruitment	✓	Career Breaks	✓
Monitoring	✓	Jobshares	✓
Positive Action	✗	Flexible Hours	✓

In 1983 the Halifax adopted an equal opportunities policy which,
as Richard Sherrard, Head of Equal Opportunities, put it:
'Formalised the fact that we want to develop fair employment
practices.' He now says the effects are beginning to show: 'It's a
two-way thing. The attitude of the organisation has to change as
do the attitudes and expectations of female staff. Both are
changing.'

The concrete effects of the policy can be felt throughout the
society. In recruitment, the numbers of women hired into
management grades are slowly increasing. Mr Sherrard says:
'Personnel concentrate on skills and ability, not gender, colour or
even academic qualifications. We use skills-based assessment and
skills-based selection.'

A clear philosophy underpins Mr Sherrard's work and this has
led to changes in policy: 'I believe all people are different and you
have to accept the differences and develop policies so that the

differences don't disadvantage people. The differences between males and females are obvious but not always appreciated in career terms. In 1983, I believe there was some scepticism about the equal opportunities policy, but now we are making progress and there is a business case for equal opportunities. I don't think the clock will turn back.'

Penny Bird, the Area Manager for Canterbury, had her two children before the society reviewed its policies: 'They were terrific. I came back after three months with each one. When I first returned everyone was supportive and I realised I had coped, so I decided it would be a good idea to have another one quick. After I came back from my second, I told my boss that I had had my children now and would like to be promoted and within six months I was. I haven't looked back since.

'I don't see promotion for women as a problem, only an individual's ability will hold them back.'

Ms Bird had exceptional support at home. Her husband took seven years off to look after the children and is now in education, so works term-times only. Even so, she has always tried to get home in time to bath the children and put them to bed, only going back to work after that: 'There is a pressure on me with the children because of not wanting to miss out. I've occasionally missed the odd nativity play. Business does come first, but the society is understanding about people with families and the need to support their children in school activities.'

For any women having babies now, there are a number of choices within the society: a career break scheme, or – for those wanting to come back – jobsharing or flexible working. As always, flexible hours are found mostly in the lower grades but there are jobshares in management.

Christina O'Donovan-Rossa, Assistant Regional Personnel Manager for the Greater London Region, is another successful woman recruit: 'In Halifax terms I'm doing well, I've leapfrogged up the scale.'

There are still no female members of the board and there are few women at the top, while the lower grades remain female-dominated. Although action is being taken to increase the rate of change.

The Halifax puts a lot of effort into education and training. Richard Sherrard says they are now looking at women returners: 'We are aware that women returners are going to be a significant part of our workforce. We must find out their particular needs and match what the Halifax can offer to those needs. We know there will be a lack of confidence so we shall develop induction around that. We are going to develop a programme specifically for women to overcome difficulties. We are actively doing research on the subject.'

Mr Sherrard believes a good equal opportunities policy pays enormous dividends: 'In terms of projecting the organisation, one can't put a price on it, but quality people apply to the organisations with the best reputation and we want quality people working for us.'

And the key is recruitment: 'If we get the selection right, attracting the people who will do the job right, they will bring the right performance. Having the right people with the right skills in the right job justifies any expense of an equal opportunities policy. When you get the wrong people, it is very expensive. If equal opportunities is inherent then it saves you a lot of money. We are doing a validation on our clerical selection and I believe it is going to show that it has saved the society significant amounts of money. The best retention strategy is to get your recruitment right.'

The Halifax has realised that equal opportunities make good business sense and that mothers have a lot to give the company. Women are slowly getting promoted - this is happening much faster in the south than the north of the country. The Halifax says this is not a matter of regional prejudice but turnover is higher in the south so there are more opportunities there than in the north. The building society has not got an outstanding record in promoting equal opportunities but it is making steady progress.

Legal & General was founded in 1836 by six lawyers who met regularly at a coffee-house in Fleet Street in London. They began by offering life assurance policies only to other lawyers, then they widened their operations. In 1989 the Legal & General had an income of £2.7 billion and was managing £17.3 billion. Its dealings now include financial services, pensions, investments, property and general insurance. It is divided into business units with head offices in London, Kingswood and Leatherhead in Surrey, Hove in Sussex and Milton Keynes in Buckinghamshire. It has offices throughout the UK. The overseas head offices are in Sydney, Washington DC, New York, Amsterdam and Paris. Legal & General has 6,700 employees in the UK; almost half of these are women.

Legal & General

Equal Opps Policy	✓	Crèche	✗
Equal Opps Recuitment	✓	Career Breaks	✓
Monitoring	✓	Jobshares	✓
Positive Action	✗	Flexible Hours	✓

The drive for equal opportunities in Legal & General comes from the top. The Chief Executive, Joe Palmer, is a big wheel on many committees concerning women at work and he wants his company to be in the forefront of employers with good working practices and good results. Legal & General is also concerned about the demographic time bomb when there will not be enough school leavers to fill vacancies, and the problem of recruiting in the south-east of the country, so as the Group Personnel Manager Geoff Smith puts it: 'We want women to know where we stand.'

A growing concern among management about the position of women in the company was turned into action in 1986 when they commissioned an equal opportunities audit by the City Business School. Geoff Smith says: 'They came out with many recommendations, and they directly changed the application forms and recruitment procedures.'

The company is divided into separate business units for its different operations. In many cases, this leads to different personnel policies, but there are also group-wide policies, including the equal opportunities policy. Initiatives in individual units may lead to a company-wide policy. For instance, two units started career break schemes and the success of these has led to the adoption of a company-wide scheme.

More and more women are being recruited, although men still tend to be in most of the top positions. As increasing numbers of women are coming through in professional areas, like computing and accounting, they are more likely to break into management. Women in senior management include the Head of the Computer Division, the Public Relations Director, the Director of Strategic Planning, the Taxation Manager, the Personnel Manager in the investments division and a director in the investments department.

Over the last decade there has been an increasing commitment to training. Dr Penny Childs, the Management Development Adviser, organises training and education for most senior managers and employees who are expected to get to that level. She says there has always been technical training but it has broadened so that there are now courses on developing personal and social skills at all levels of the company.

Dr Childs notes that effort put into training and development has come particularly in the last few years, together with the increasing opportunities for women: 'The company has changed since I joined in 1984, particularly in what it is prepared to do for women and the expectation of women. Now there's an assumption career women will come back after having children.'

Dr Childs is a single mother of a young child and leaving the office at 5 p.m. every day to get home and relieve her nanny has changed her working pattern, as she used to do very irregular hours: 'It requires a fair amount of effort and a lot of organisation; the problem is almost as much a sense of guilt as a practical problem. The company has been very co-operative and supportive.

'I think it's more accepted now that when women have very

young children, their hours are restricted. I have been promoted
since I've been back from maternity leave, but I would not be
considered for certain jobs; that's the price I have to pay.'

Sue Wallis, secretary to the Communications Director, is about
to go on maternity leave; she was bowled over by the support she
was given when she announced her pregnancy: 'They're great,
Everybody took the news very well. I didn't have to make any
difficult decisions about when I was coming back. I'm entitled to
nearly seven months off, but I might take only three.'

Val Arnold, a Senior Computer Auditor in Kingswood, Surrey,
who is on maternity leave with her second child agrees the
company is very helpful during pregnancy: 'During my first
maternity leave they were very positive and willing to give me a
bit of work to do from home: I got paid for whatever hours I
managed. I kept my old job part-time, doing mostly mornings only.
I wouldn't have gone back if they had made me work full-time; I
wanted to spend some time with my boy. I would have looked
elsewhere. I was the first part-timer in Audit. They are very keen
to accommodate people's needs and will give individual contracts
to suit hours.'

Ms Arnold may have been a mould breaker, but her individual
contract is no longer unusual. Kingswood leads the way in the
company with individual contracts that are tailored to suit
individual needs. The company is moving towards meeting the
EEC Directive on Part-timers (see page 266) so that the benefits
and pay full-timers are entitled to will be paid on a pro rata basis
to part-timers.

There is also the benefit of Legal & General's enhanced
maternity package for mothers who return to work. For most
women, like Sue Wallis, there is a 25 per cent supplement in salary
for the first six months after returning, plus holiday accrued
during maternity leave. More senior women like Val Arnold get
eighteen weeks full pay, plus accrued holiday.

The maternity package is available to any woman working for the
company, however briefly she has been there. Geoff Smith explained the philosophy: 'If we want to hire someone, it's a long-term
commitment. It doesn't matter whether they are eight months
pregnant when they join. They are still entitled to all our benefits.'

Ms Arnold joined Legal & General in 1977 and has seen great changes: 'About 1983, more women began to come back after maternity leave. There are more women in senior positions, and I have never come across any prejudice. They're very keen on equal opportunities.

'I've got to the level where I am happy and I don't want to go into management. I can work by myself, which suits me. I spent a year or two as a Project Leader, but I didn't really enjoy it: it was getting other people to do work, but I want to do it myself.'

Legal & General is showing its commitment to changing past practices through proper training and opportunities, negotiating individual hours and enhanced maternity benefits. For companies, like Legal & General, who are dependent on hiring - and retaining - skilled people in the south-east of England, this way of operating will become the norm rather than the exception.

The Midland Bank is one of the Big Four British clearing banks. The headquarters are in London, but it has branches and payment services centres throughout the UK. Over half the employees of the Midland Bank are women.

Midland Bank

Equal Opps Policy	✓	Crèche	✓
Equal Opps Recruitment	✓	Career Breaks	✓
Monitoring	✓	Jobshares	✓
Positive Action	✓	Flexible Hours	✓

The Midland Bank is famous for its nationwide network of nurseries. By the end of 1991, there will be 124 nurseries in operation along with thirty holiday playschemes. While this has attracted publicity, it is but part of a wider equal opportunities package. The many initiatives, including career breaks, jobsharing and special training, were good enough to make the bank a finalist in the Women In Management (WIM) Equal Opportunity Employer Awards. WIM is an organisation support group for women in management and those aspiring to management; it is dedicated to raising the quality of managerial practices.

In 1988 the Midland appointed its first Equal Opportunities Director, Anne Watts, who has reviewed all staff policy.

The Midland does not only want to attract women: it wants to retain them and make it possible for them to mix a career with children. Recruitment is important – the bank has recently revised its application form and reviews all its recruitment literature regularly. It is constantly monitored. The number and distribution of women is analysed along with the figures for promotion training and progress on implementing its equal opportunities policy.

Sadie Muskett joined the graduate training scheme three years ago because she was so impressed with the bank and is now a

Branch Manager in Cambridge. Among her potential employers, only the Midland did not mind that she was engaged to be married and so would not be able to be posted anywhere in the country. The bank guaranteed that her personal circumstances would be taken into account when they were deciding where to place her. She also liked the childcare policies: 'As with my female colleagues, I looked at the childcare arrangements because in your early twenties you cannot rule out what will happen to you in the mid-thirties. I believe a nursery is coming to the Cambridge area soon, I would be happy to produce a couple of kids to have in there.

'What I like about the Midland is that if I got pregnant tomorrow it would be personally inconvenient, but my career would not fall around my ears. It would be a minor hiccup to the bank. If I wanted three years off it would be no problem. It is a comforting thought.'

The Midland has brought in a two-tier career break scheme for mothers who do not want to return to full-time work immediately. There is a Priority Returners Scheme for clerical staff, keeping them in touch with the bank, offering opportunities to update their skills and giving them priority when they wish to return. There is also a Retainer Scheme, which is open to staff on managerial grades or management training schemes, that guarantees a return to the same grade. Both schemes encourage women to take up part-time work whilst on the break.

Jane Murphy, a Corporate Banking Officer in Cardiff, has been on the retainer scheme since the birth of 2-year-old Ian. She was a full-time mother but after fifteen months she found she was getting depressed and her doctor advised her to return to work. Now she does two days a week. She says: 'I'm a changed woman since I have gone back to work. My parents and my husband all say so. I like to think I've got the best of both worlds as no way would I have gone back full-time.'

Ms Murphy joined eighteen years ago at the age of 16: 'I joined as a job to get out of school. After twelve months, I thought there's got to be more than this. My manager encouraged me to take banking exams. They were the be all and end all. Men had to have banking exams, but women were not even mentioned. I was lucky to have a manager to encourage me, then I moved on quite quickly.

But the Personnel Manager at the time was not at all for women. At my annual interview the first question was: "When are you going to get married?" Then: "When are you going to have a baby?" Doors were not particularly open, you had to push them yourself. You had to be twice as good as any man to be noticed. The Regional Director said I shouldn't be at work, I should be at home running W.I. meetings like his wife.'

Ms Murphy became the first woman manager in Wales and the bank was transformed: 'Things are much better. There's a hell of a difference between then and now. I know two women jobsharing teams. Five years ago this wasn't available.'

June Boylin is another school leaver who has risen up the hierarchy. Twenty-two years on she is Regional Operations Manager for the North of England. The job is demanding and she combines it with bringing up two children of 4 and 7, and a 120-mile daily commute because the office was relocated from Manchester to Leeds and she did not want to disrupt the family. She reckons on being at the office by 7.30 a.m. and leaving at 6 p.m., so she is home in time to see the children. After they have gone to bed she pulls out her work for the rest of the evening and puts some hours in most weekends. She says: 'I try to balance it as best I can.'

Ms Boylin has nothing but praise for the bank: 'I have always been treated extremely well by the Midland. It is a superb employer. There was no problem promoting me with children. It didn't form part of the decision at all. I've had quite a few promotions and my bosses only found out I had the children after I was given the job.'

Now there is the opportunity for more structured training for young women like Ms Boylin and Ms Murphy who leave school with few qualifications and who want to move into management. A year-long business diploma, on full pay, at one of five universities or colleges around the country has been successful. In 1989-90, there were fifty people on the course, forty of them women. In 1990-1, sixty-seven out of the eighty attending were women.

For other women there are courses to help them with career and life planning and to develop management skills. The bank is supporting a network of women called 'Women in Midland' which meets on a monthly basis in London. The group's objectives are to assist women in developing their career potential and to increase their sense of involvement in the Midland Group.

Graduate women on management training schemes are expected to perform as well as the men. Sadie Muskett says: 'The bank has always treated me fairly but I feel it will take a few years for the policy in action now to be felt throughout the bank. Graduate women make themselves heard, but there is a big dilemma further down for clerical employees, because it tends to be men who get on. The pattern is for the majority of clerical workers to be women and the managers to be men.'

The accusation that the high-flying women are well looked after while the vast majority of clerical workers are not, has echoes throughout the finance industry. Midland has recently introduced a career and development training initiative aimed at women in clerical grades called Springboard. Springboard helps women reassess where they want to go and empowers them to take action.

Most progressive organisations have policies like career breaks which apply to all staff instead of differentiating between staff and management grades. However, the Midland has certainly gone a long way in its drive to give women equal opportunities, and the massive nursery programme it has undertaken shows it is prepared to put money up as well as fine words.

National Westminster Bank has branches throughout the UK.
The bank is involved in three operational areas: UK
Financial Services; Corporate and Institutional banking; and
International Businesses which incorporates retail banking
businesses in the USA and Europe as well as associates in
Australia. There are some 78,000 employees, almost 60 per
cent of whom are women.

National Westminster Bank PLC

Equal Opps Policy	✓	Crèche	✗
Equal Opps Recruitment	✓	Career Breaks	✓
Monitoring	✓	Jobshares	✓
Positive Action	✓	Flexible Hours	✓

The year 1980 was the turning point for women in the National
Westminster Bank. There was a review of their situation, followed
by a positive action plan. The philosophy behind the programme
was communicated to all employees and publicly supported by the
highest levels of management. The directors stressed that this was
a serious long-term strategy and part of the bank's overall
manpower planning initiative.

A women's workshop was arranged: fifteen employees with
identified potential took part in a think tank about the position of
female staff and provided a comprehensive report on the way to
proceed. Their findings were used in the development of the equal
opportunities initiatives subsequently implemented. Following
the publication of the review, a Career Planning Manager for
Women was appointed – this job description has since been
widened to an Equal Opportunities Manager who heads a unit of
four staff. Within each sector, division and region, a Personnel
Manager has been trained and designated with specific
responsibility for equal opportunity issues.

The bank sends women on a special Management Development

for Women training course aimed at potential high-flyers. This course emphasises participants' development and makes sure their training is not just a matter of personal development *per se* but also fits in with the requirements of the organisation. The introduction of the management development programme has ensured more objective selection of staff for development and more rapid advancement for those with potential, ensuring equal opportunities for women.

Angela Sheen, the Recruitment Manager for London, has obviously benefited from the bank's encouragement of women. Now in her forties, she joined in 1964, leaving to have a baby in 1968; she then rejoined in 1971 and worked on a part-time basis until 1977 when she became full-time. When she returned after her children she 'almost started at the bottom again' and was seen more as a mother than anything else. Since 1980, she has been getting promotion after promotion – sometimes jumping two grades: 'I've no complaints, once they caught on to the fact that I wanted a career, it was very fast.

'The opportunities are there, but it depends slightly where you go. The further west and further north you go attitudes are different. Sometimes the women are not grasping the opportunities on offer, while in some areas they are not encouraged enough.'

Annette Broadbent started in a Leicester branch as a school leaver, just looking on it as a job rather than a career. She was not expected to take her banking exams or to progress beyond a certain level. When she moved to London, to follow her husband, all this changed: 'My management encouraged me to take exams and go for promotion.'

She is now an Assistant Manager in a London branch with about 400 staff. She has also returned from a five-year career break – half of which was part-time working: 'I wanted to see my little boy settled, I enjoyed being at home with him during his formative years. Without a career break I would have certainly taken my maternity leave and then resigned, although I would have eventually come back to work.

'I'm very positive about the scheme. I was given encouragement to come back and lots of help. The part-time work kept me in touch with the bank. The hours were flexible and I was at the same level as I had been before I took my break. I have even been promoted since coming back.'

Patricia English, who is in her mid-twenties and was part of the bank's graduate intake in 1986, is more dubious about career breaks and their effect on a career: 'When it comes down to it, three or four years off won't do you any favours. It is a long time, particularly if you want to get to the top.'

When she has children, she intends to take a break but has counted herself out from reaching executive status: 'I think I could go to the top if I wanted to, but I don't want to go that far. It's something I feel within me. I want an interesting career – doing a variety of things. But to reach the very top you have to be truly devoted. Those people have no time at all outside their work.'

Ms English is the Assistant Manager of the Corporate Affairs Department. She has been promoted twice since going to Nat West. She went on one of the career development courses and was full of praise for it: 'I went for a week and had to write my own report, looking at my future and identifying the jobs I want to do. I have worked out where I would like my next move to be.'

She says that for graduates there are equal chances for men and women, but for the less qualified staff there is a difference in achievement, due partly to women's lack of confidence in their own abilities.

Certainly in the early 1980s equal opportunities were aimed at the graduate high-flyers, but now all women benefit. Sean Dixon from the Equal Opportunities Unit says the bank realises that a 16 year old who chooses to join the bank can be just as intelligent as the young woman who chooses to continue her education: 'It is not unusual for someone who has come in with just 'O' levels to be on a higher grade six years later than the graduate who is joining.'

*The Prudential is Britain's largest life insurance and
financial services group. Its head office is based in London
and it has over 400 offices around the UK. It employs 25,000
people, over a third of them are women.*

Prudential Corporation

Equal Opps Policy	✓	Crèche	✓
Equal Opps Recruitment	✓	Career Breaks	✓
Monitoring	✓	Jobshares	✓
Positive Action	✓	Flexible Hours	✓

The Prudential has shaken off its stuffy, 'man from the Pru' image
and gone into equal opportunities with a bang. It certainly had a
lot of changing to do.

When Jean White joined twenty-one years ago at the age of 16,
women did not even get concessionary rates for staff mortgages.
They now keep their concessionary rates while on maternity leave.
In those days women could not work on the commercial side
because, as one man explained to her, 'women wouldn't know what
a five mortice Chubb lock was'.

Ms White worked for five years in the Accounts Department and
then became a District Agent in Stanmore, Middlesex, which was
unusual for a woman at the time: 'I chose Stanmore because there
were four or five lady agents and I felt I wouldn't be on my own.'

She found that having her son, Peter, was an incentive for
getting on rather than having the opposite effect: 'I was
encouraged to go for promotion after I had my son, probably
because he made me a lot more organised. I put it off until he was
5. I am now a Section Manager and am being encouraged to go
for District Manager, probably because I was so late getting my
first promotion. My son made me more serious about the job; he
gave me a purpose.'

Although 51 per cent of office staff are women, they only make up 28 per cent of field staff. Karen Lock has experienced both sides of the Pru. When she was pregnant five years ago, she was on a course which meant being seconded to various departments. While many of the managers congratulated her and put her to work, one of them actually wrote to the management that he thought she was wasting her time and the company's money.

The Pensions Department was so impressed with her when she had returned to them after maternity leave that she has been promoted to Senior Pensions Administrator. Her son, Tristram, is in the company crèche, about a mile away from where she works in Reading. She says: 'Full marks to the Pru for doing that. I haven't come across anybody who doesn't like it. I think it's really important, quite a big step for a company to take.'

Both women returned to work full-time, but there are a variety of options open to women, through a career break, jobsharing and other part-time arrangements, to working at home when this can be arranged. Term-time working and annual hours contracts are also under consideration for particular locations or occupational groups.

The Pru has a variety of training courses including Career Development for Women, a women-only residential course run four times a year. Ms Lock took this course and found it helpful: 'For a start everybody there wanted to be on it. It was for women in management, to teach you skills and give you ideas, like how to be assertive.'

The Pru has begun to look at the barriers to women in the organisation. Only 5.6 per cent of senior management are female. Ms White says: 'There are still District Managers who think that women ought to be at home looking after the children. Until we get more women in senior management, over say 10 per cent, it will be very difficult for women to be truly recognised.'

The Pru recognises this problem. In fact, Ms White says: 'If anything the opportunities are better for me than for a man now, because the Pru is trying to be positive to combat the low percentage of women.' She is not so sure about the company's motives: 'I'm not sure whether they feel we're going to do a good job or they need more staff. Realistically they need more skilled people.'

In her department she is trying to encourage more women into the job, by targeting advertisements towards women: 'Now it's just word of mouth and until you get more ladies in the job, that will only attract men.'

She is also aware of how positive action can alienate men: 'I did start a ladies group for the agents, because there were thirty ladies out of 500 men, and the ladies thought it was wonderful. But some of the men thought it was elitist and asked why we were doing it for the ladies and not for them, so we stopped it. It was a shame. I would have liked to take it further, because it could have encouraged ladies into the job.'

Overall she says the Pru really has pulled its socks up: 'Now they make sure the opportunities are there and it's up to you whether you take them. When I first got here there were no opportunities.'

The Prudential has dealt well with the mechanics of equal opportunity: instituting flexible working for women, crèche places and trying to attract more women into the organisation. Now it is a matter of changing entrenched attitudes so women are given a fair crack at the whip.

The Royal Bank of Scotland offers a full range of financial
services from simple overdrafts to major corporate syndicate
loans. It has its headquarters in Edinburgh and has branches
throughout the UK. The bank employs 21,000 people, 12,000 of
whom are women. Women work in all areas of the bank from
marketing and PR to the many posts in a branch, including
some managers, and computer operations.

Royal Bank of Scotland

Equal Opps Policy	✓	Crèche	✗
Equal Opps Recruitment	✓	Career Breaks	✓
Monitoring	✓	Jobshares	✓
Positive Action	✗	Flexible Hours	✓

The Royal Bank of Scotland is not going to be left behind by the
London-based banks and is working hard to improve career
opportunities for women. It has appointed an Equal Opportunities
Manager, Jane Barber, to help it achieve success, not only for
women but also for people from ethnic minority communities and
people with disabilities.

Although the bank has made progress it certainly needs Jane
Barber. There is only one woman on the all-white board and there
are no women in senior management. Eighteen per cent of junior
and middle management are women. There has been an overhaul
of recruitment and promotion policy, which is monitored to ensure
that it is working. Awareness training and selection techniques
have been introduced and updated. By 1990, 75 per cent of all
graduate recruits were female, 5 per cent up on 1989, as well as
60 per cent of the school leavers.

Lesley Skinner was one of the school leavers who arrived ten
years ago. She wanted to have a career rather than a job. She was
16 and was qualified to go onto further education, but she chose
to work. The bank encouraged her to do her banking exams on day

release for her Part I course and two periods of block release for
Part II, which it paid for. She is now a Bank Supervisor in the West
End branch in Aberdeen and is confident she will go on being
promoted.

Ms Skinner completed her exams more quickly than many of her
male colleagues and she says she has not suffered any
discrimination. She believes there have been many changes for the
better: 'Now the bank says it has a non-discriminatory policy, such
things are discussed more. There are changes, women are staying
on much more after having children.

'What women need today are genuine options. The bank is
recognising this need and coming up with suggestions. Then they
won't lose as many people to have families as in the past.'

Ms Skinner intends to have children and welcomes the career
break of up to five years for the care of children or of ill or elderly,
dependent relatives. People on career breaks can take the time off
or work part-time during their breaks. She says: 'Part-time used
to mean having to do basic clerical duties, but the career break
means you can go part-time and not lose your status.'

Trish Gray, a Systems Development Manager in Edinburgh, had
her two boys before the career break policy was introduced. She
resigned to have Andrew eight years ago, but when he was 18
months old, her former manager rang and asked her to go back
part-time on a temporary basis. Fifteen months later, she left
again to have Stuart, returning again on a part-time basis and
going back to full-time three years ago.

She would have appreciated the career break: 'That policy
transformed things. It allowed people to take time out and not
resign to go part-time. Part-time posts are now being created and
we could get permanent part-time positions. Three people in my
office are on career break at present and no one treats it as
strange.'

Trish Gray pioneered changing the policy on part-timers, so that
women do not just have temporary, low-status jobs but can
continue their careers on a part-time basis. She was the first part-
timer in her section of the bank's computing department and,
while she was away having Stuart, everything changed because
new equal opportunities initiatives began to be implemented.

About 200 women have begun a career break scheme since it was launched in 1989, which has lead to an increase in part-time working among quite senior staff. Hours are agreed with staff to suit individual requirements whenever possible. There are pro rata benefits for part-time staff.

What pleases Ms Gray is that she has been promoted several times since her return and has become one of the most senior women in her department: 'I've been fairly lucky since I've been back. I would say I hold my correct place.'

Although maternity pay and leave is still the statutory minimum, the bank perk of a subsidised mortgage is retained as long as staff return for six months after maternity leave.

Certainly efforts are being made by the bank to encourage women to join and to stay. There were only eight women in Trish Gray's section when she joined, now almost a quarter of the staff there are women. She says: 'As far as the bank is concerned, it will be reasonable to a working woman with children as long as she is reasonable with the bank. But if you are going to get ahead as a woman in the bank when you are at work you have to be a banker not a mother.'

Until women get into senior management and achieve large numbers in junior and middle management the bank cannot afford to rest on its laurels. However, the equal opportunity initiatives are quite clearly having an effect in the growing numbers of women getting into management. They also allow women to plan a career with the bank that will not be brought to a halt when they want to take some time off to care for children. The Equal Opportunities Manager, Jane Barber, has shown just what can be achieved with good policies and receptive directors in the short time she has been in her post since the beginning of 1989.

*Sun Life of Canada is a Canadian Life Assurance company
with its British headquarters in Basingstoke, Hampshire. In
1990, it was the winner of the* New Woman *magazine Best
Company for Women competition. It employs 1,070 people, 700
of them women.*

Sun Life of Canada

Equal Opps Policy	✓	Crèche	✗
Equal Opps Recruitment	✓	Career Breaks	✗
Monitoring	✗	Jobshares	✓
Positive Action	✗	Flexible Hours	✓

When Sun Life of Canada moved its headquarters from central
London to Basingstoke the company gained the impetus to
examine and improve the terms and conditions of its employees.
The Thames Valley is an area of skills shortages and Sun Life
knew it would need a major recruitment drive to replace the
people who had chosen to stay in London.

Andrea Spencer is Compensation and Benefits Manager and
made the move with the company: 'Since we have been down in
Basingstoke, women have been high on the agenda. Rather than
getting statements or policies, it's an attitude of mind. Our whole
recruitment strategy has changed. When we came here, there was
a demographics problem, so the policy had to change. We had to
ask ourselves what kind of people do we want? Are our jobs being
done by those sort of people?

'We had to change management attitudes. Now, we don't look
for qualifications, we look at what you need for the job. We can
attract mature shop assistants, they are more stable and more
than capable – particularly if we offer them flexible working
hours.'

There is a realisation in the company that women with few
educational qualifications who have not pursued a career but have

brought up a family can offer a great deal. Ms Spencer says: 'We had one lady who had been a cook, working for us. She was doing a wonderful job. The manager wanted to promote her but she hadn't got the required A levels. She was promoted and has been in the job twelve months and is one of the best we've got.'

When Ms Spencer joined Sun Life of Canada seven years ago, she saw it as a short-term career move: 'As my previous job did not give me training, I thought I would get that and some experience, but I did not intend to relocate. However, the company is receptive to change and I would rather work in a small organisation where I can contribute and gain a lot. I am able to have an impact right up to the top – to the board in Canada.'

The company has done much to make it easy for people with outside commitments, particularly mothers, by having flexi-time as standard for all employees. A childcare register has been set up giving all the local area's registered childminders. The company is also looking into the feasibility of a childcare vouchers system. This works in the same way as luncheon vouchers work: childcare vouchers are given out by employers and are then redeemable against childcare services.

Sun Life offers a variety of flexible hours contracts, jobsharing, term-time working and part-time arrangements. It is contemplating introducing home-working. None of this is company policy yet, because, Ms Spencer says: 'We like to try it in practice before putting it in as policy. One of the qualities about personnel in this company is that – we try to test ideas out.'

Karen Gunther is a Personnel Services Administrator who has been with Sun Life for ten years. She has been working two days a week since returning after the birth of her son, Greg: 'I thought about going back full-time, but I felt it was too much of a step to take. I did not want to fail either at work or as a mother. I'm taking things gradually and it's working really well. I even get the full range of benefits: a mortgage subsidy, free pension and free group life cover.'

Ms Gunther says there have been no problems. In fact, when she went on maternity leave, she was offered part-time work to come back to and she still retains her old status: 'I expect to go on doing interesting work and using my knowledge and skills. I don't expect the dumpy work no one else wants to do. It would be a waste of money, because, pro rata, I'm on the same salary as when I left.'

She feels the company gains from the arrangement as well as her: 'I love working two days a week – it's a rest. I'm full of energy for work and after my two days I'm much more enthusiastic about the baby and do much more with him.'

The other focus of change is getting more women into management. Ms Spencer says: 'They want to increase the numbers of senior women both for sound business reasons and social pressures. My immediate boss positively went out and made himself aware of women's issues. We are part of the local employers' Women and Industry group.'

As with all financial institutions, Sun Life of Canada is bottom heavy with women: over two-thirds of graded staff are women, while in management it is less than one sixth – fifteen women and sixty-eight men. Linda Mizen is an Underwriting Manager who has two small children. She experiences no particular problems mixing work and motherhood. One great help is that the hours she is expected to work are reasonable – mostly 9 a.m. to 6 p.m. – although in October all the rules get broken because it is a particularly busy month. Flexi-time means that if she works nine hours for three days she can take a day off. Although this puts her childcare arrangements out of kilter, her children still see a lot of her. She regularly travels to the USA and Canada, but is given enough warning to make arrangements for the children.

She says she has noticed many changes in her five years with the company: 'The concept of equal opportunities is moving up the ranks. There are not many women higher than me in the company, but to some extent getting women up there is a matter of time. It used to be very male. I think there are no blocks on women going up. I don't think I would not be considered for a post just because I was a woman.'

She, too, sees the future in increased flexible working: 'In this department we are looking at jobshares and have split one job into two part-time jobs. The company is quite prepared to support that arrangement. I think that's the way we shall be going.'

Apparently, the directors of the company were amazed when they won the *New Woman* magazine award. Far from resting on their laurels, it has spurred the managers on to do more, so now all policies are being examined to improve them further.

*TSB Retail Banking, formerly known as Trustee Savings
Bank, is responsible for TSB banking operations in England,
Wales, Scotland, Northern Ireland and the Channel Islands,
along with related banking services. It operates through a
network of over 1,500 branches dealing with savings and
deposits, plastic cards, loans and mortgages. The retail
banking head offices are moving to Birmingham, from
London, in early 1992. TSB employs over 25,000 staff, over 60
per cent of whom are women.*

TSB

Equal Opps Policy	✓	Crèche	✓
Equal Opps Recruitment	✓	Career Breaks	✓
Monitoring	✓	Jobshares	✓
Positive Action	✓	Flexible Hours	✓

TSB came late into the Equal Opportunities fold, later than many
other companies in the financial sector. It set up its Equal
Opportunities Steering Group only in September 1990, but the
programme is extraordinarily thorough and its first phase 'action
plans' are due to be completed by Spring 1992.

All senior executives have participated in strategic planning
seminars on equal opportunities, and management training on
equal opportunities will be cascaded throughout the organisation.
The composition of the workforce by race, sex and disability is
reviewed by senior management on a quarterly and annual basis.

TSB has changed its advertising style for junior entrants to
attract a broader range of applicants, including women returning
to work after having children. Selection and promotion methods
are being reviewed, recruiters trained and decisions monitored.

Parents will not be excluded. Those who come back part-time
receive full pro rata benefits, including a mortgage subsidy and
pensions. There is a career break scheme for staff with children

or other domestic responsibilities. The new head office in
Birmingham has a nursery and the bank is considering other
measures to help staff effectively combine work and domestic
responsibilities.

Judith Shaikh, one of the few senior women managers, says
there have been many changes for the good in her fifteen years
with the bank: 'I came in just before the Equal Pay Act became
law, when they did not even give women mortgages. Even now,
there are some male bosses who have the reputation of not liking
women in management, but it's more a matter of personality than
a company problem.

'Things have definitely changed – partly as a result of pressure
from outside and partly because of good women in the company.
Because there are more women around, the bank is trying to take
the best people available – it makes good business sense. I
suspect, too, that since some of the old guard retired, my
generation began to hook into the opportunities.'

Ms Shaikh has always had steady advancement but the future
is not so certain: 'The promotion prospects are unclear possibly
because I'm not sure how far I want to go. It's partly a matter
of personal choice and partly my background and experience,
which is in accountancy and strategic planning, not the branches.
That could hold me back. On the other hand, a lot of women who
have risen are specialists.

'If I were asked to be a director, I'm still ambitious enough to
want it, but I would have to think seriously about my other
commitments – my husband, who has taken early retirement. I
would be flattered to be offered it.'

Another change Ms Shaikh has noticed is that staff can now plan
a family and career. Dawn Hughes is a Clerical Supervisor in the
Bishop Auckland branch. She has taken up the parental leave
scheme for five years after the birth of 7-month-old Jonathan. The
scheme is flexible and she has chosen to work two days a week:
'It's made everything easier. The two days back at work are like
a holiday, because Jonathan is quite a difficult baby, and the rest
of the week I enjoy staying at home with him.'

She would not have gone back full-time: 'I'm pleased I was
pregnant at the right time, but they must have wasted thousands

and thousands of pounds on training women who could not go back to work because they could not manage full-time.'

Julie Rodwell, the Branch Manager in Bletchley, came back full-time after having Emma two years ago. She had taken five months maternity leave: 'It has been much easier than I expected. Very occasionally I take work home with me and meetings outside working hours take some juggling, but my parents live nearby and can pick her up from the childminder. I was Manager before Emma was born and did not see why it should hold me back.'

Ms Rodwell joined at 16, straight from school, and has been able to work her way up: 'I always looked at it as a career. Some people took me seriously and some didn't. My first manager was one of the old guard, but I joined at the same time as two young lads who did day release and I wanted to do it too, so he let me.

'Very soon after that I was transferred to another branch where I was given every encouragement. The positive reaction did help.'

She has noticed changes since joining in 1976: 'There were fairly few women in management positions, but they are not such a rarity now. The general attitude has improved. The bank has made efforts to encourage women to progress. I have never been held back, and certain managers have given me great encouragement.'

The bank is introducing targets in promotion and recruitment and women should be able to make great strides.

TSB has moved fast, certainly its policies are now in line with the best companies in the financial sector. It has appointed an Equal Opportunities Manager, Julie Mellor, to show it means business. The prospects are good.

HIGH-TECH

Bull is a French/American computer company which designs, manufactures, markets and sells computer solutions and services. The UK Head Office is in Brentford, Middlesex, and it has major centres and offices throughout the UK. It employs 2,500 people, almost a quarter of whom are women.

Bull HN Information Systems Ltd

Equal Opps Policy	✓	Crèche	✗
Equal Opps Recruitment	✓	Career Breaks	✓
Monitoring	✗	Jobshares	✓
Positive Action	✗	Flexible Hours	✓

For an information technology company Bull has surprisingly few women employees. Many of the technical areas have consequently become rather masculine enclaves. In the hierarchy, most women are firmly in junior positions: women make up 9 per cent of management and 4 per cent of senior management, and there are no women on the board.

The problem begins with the small number of women applying for jobs with the company, in spite of the equal opportunities policy covering advertising for jobs, recruitment and selection. Kim Lambert, the Manager of Software Development in Hemel Hempstead, says Bull does not seem to attract graduate women applicants: 'I interview and recruit but I rarely see any women. I think the company should think about why women aren't applying. According to an analysis of the figures there are less female applicants now than five or six years ago. That is making them take the problem seriously.'

Ms Lambert says she joined because 'the guy that interviewed me was so enthusiastic'. As a graduate she was put on the fast track and after eleven years she is now one of the most senior women in Bull: 'I've done quite well. Because it's high-tech it doesn't seem to matter that much whether you are a man or a woman: it's whether you can do the job.'

However, she sees going much further as impossible: 'All the senior management in Bull are men – I can't see that changing. The very senior management are entrenched in old ideas. I can't see myself getting up there. There are two reasons why: there's a lot of competition for the few available jobs and there is a reluctance on behalf of some senior management in Bull to promote women.

'If I do get stuck, I shall probably leave. I might move sideways and do something different in the organisation. More likely I would like to join an affiliate company in France or the USA, where there are a lot of senior women.'

Marcia Cotton is another successful woman in Bull. After seven years with the company she is the Manager of Marketing Communications: 'My boss left when I was on maternity leave and I was offered the job. I was very surprised because even if you're out of the loop for a few months, out of sight is out of mind. I feel I've been lucky, I've not got a degree, but I've done better than many other people.' She puts most of her success down to communications departments being traditionally good to women, but believes: 'Bull has a long way to go in developing women. Their record on promoting women is questionable. They don't have many women in management positions. Why? Either because they're employing the wrong women or not promoting them.'

She is one of the few mothers in such a senior position and ensures that her work is always up to standard: 'It is exceptional to work late evenings but I do work more than forty hours – further down the loop it is easier to work shorter hours. I'm not disciplined and I always work late, so my child suffers. The pressure is personal – it's not the company but your workmates. You have to prove yourself as a woman then as a mother: that you are just as good as a single person.'

Residential training courses are her personal bugbear: she

boycotts them because she hates being away from home: 'I work
nine to ten hours a day, often take work home and even at the
weekends I'm preparing reports. I live and breathe work but I
draw the line at long spells away from home.'

Bull is flexible about taking into account the needs of its working
mothers. There are career breaks of up to five years, with
provisions for working part-time during that period. Jobshares
may be arranged, and home working, term-time working and
limited flexi-time are all possible.

Moira Acres, Manager of Sales Support, had 6-year-old Guy
before these policies came into effect: 'It was quite difficult. I was
a salesperson and always intended to come back to work, but found
it impossible. I wanted to come back to a technical support role
part-time. To do that I had to resign and go freelance, and could
then be offered part-time work.'

Now she is treated well. As a single mother, with her child in
an after-school nursery, she has to work fixed hours to pick him
up: 'It's no problem at all. I thought it would count against me,
but I've always been assured it doesn't. I went back full-time in
this position.

'I do worry about the future and getting promoted again. If it
happened I would almost certainly have to move to another
location. At the moment, here in Reigate, I live reasonably close
to my office, so everything is manageable.'

Ms Lambert says: 'I think Bull is trying now, but the firm did
not try very hard in the past. It was very selective about offering
help to mothers, but it now seems to have recognised over the last
year that it must make more of an effort.'

Ms Cotton is equally lukewarm about Bull's efforts: 'Overall the
company has noticed the trends and realises it has to offer more
to women, but it is not innovatory. The crèche was turned down
very easily.'

Bull offers a lot of training courses covering technical areas,
personal skills and management development. The company
encourages self-development through on-the-job training,
membership of professional institutions and assistance with
evening classes and Open University courses. Ms Lambert found
the management training courses helpful: 'Most women – like me

- lack confidence, so it helps. They have also meant I have met a lot of people throughout the company.'

Bull is a friendly company to work in and Ms Lambert says one of the reasons she enjoys her work so much is because her colleagues tend to be technically competent, high-calibre people: 'It's challenging working in that kind of environment.' Overall it is clear that women in Bull feel the company is making progress but must try harder if it is to attract its proportion of women and retain them.

*International Computers Limited is a leading European
information technology company which is part of the Fujitsu
group of companies - the world's second largest information
technology group. It manufactures and markets a variety of
information systems. Its headquarters are in London and it
has offices throughout the UK, with a lot of opportunities
abroad. The company employs 22,000 people worldwide,
almost a third of whom are women.*

International Computers Limited (ICL)

Equal Opps Policy	✓	Crèche	✗
Equal Opps Recruitment	✓	Career Breaks	✓
Monitoring	✓	Jobshares	✓
Positive Action	✗	Flexible Hours	✓

ICL was a founding member of the Women into Information
Technology Campaign which aims to attract more women into
information technology from school, university or as returning
mothers. ICL has followed up this public commitment by exploring
the barriers to women in the company, and trying to break them
down, as well as overhauling the recruitment strategy and
methods so they are not biased in favour of men. This initiative
has been so successful that a higher proportion of the women
applicants are now employed than the men, but that is still only
a quarter of all appointments. ICL knows it must attract more
women to apply in the first place. A special four-page booklet
aimed at women has been published to try and persuade them that
ICL is the company for them, and that information technology is
a career which welcomes women. Of the seven successful women
profiled in the booklet, only one is a mother, and she was a
homeworker for eight years.

Of course, the way in which ICL has pioneered homeworking is
to be commended. Rates of pay for homeworkers match the

rates for those who work in offices, and women homeworkers can continue to advance their careers by getting promoted to such positions as Team Leader, or if they are more senior, to carry on with the work they had been doing but adapt it to working from home. However, many mothers in ICL prefer to continue full-time work at their office desks. The company is certainly keen to retain its skilled women after they have had children and it is flexible in accommodating their needs.

ICL has had employees working from home for over eighteen years. This group is largely made up of experienced software development professionals, and it now numbers several hundred people. All but 5 per cent of ICL's homeworkers are women.

The badinage and support of an office is lacking for homeworkers and ICL tries to cut down on their isolation. Working alone at home does nevertheless involve considerable self-discipline. After Joan Arnold became a mother she did twenty hours a week with ICL's Contract Programming Services, the homeworking division. She slowly increased her hours. She became a Team Leader, organising other homeworkers. Managing people off-site, she says, is a particularly delicate job, because one has to be able to spot problems by the nuances in a voice: 'I was working with women going through the process of having and looking after babies, which meant there were many stresses and strains.' Later she became Project Manager, in charge of all the part-time women working for the Kidsgrove site in the Midlands.

ICL tries hard to be flexible. Employees can go on to part-time work or have other flexible arrangements to enable them to cope with domestic arrangements. The overall policy, according to the leaflet, 'recognises not only the need to provide support to working mothers but also single parents, those caring for elderly relatives or who have specific domestic problems by being sufficiently flexible to meet those needs within a group environment'.

Juliet Hancock is a Resourcing and Development Manager who went back to work three days a week after the birth of her son, James. When her husband, a vicar, moved to Derbyshire, she could no longer continue working at Basingstoke and there was no other ICL site to which she could transfer. She decided to take advantage of the career break scheme, which offers time out from the company combined with sufficient flexible work and training to keep skills up to date. She works from home on specific projects, still in her personnel and training role. She is involved in a company-wide evaluation programme and has assessed a self-development programme for homeworkers, as well as giving occasional on-site training courses.

Ms Hancock is enthusiastic about the arrangement: 'It's wonderful. I work two days a week, a lot of it is at home but I also visit ICL sites. What I'm hoping to establish is that flexible working can be successful on a long-term basis. Realistically, as long as we are based here in Derbyshire, I will not go back full-time on an on-site basis.

'I am the first person at management level to be employed on a part-time basis and formally take advantage of the career break scheme. What's happening at ICL is a reflection of what's happening as a whole. It is not benevolent, but hard-nosed good business sense and women must exploit that. A lot of women are saying to me: "Have a go. Make it easier for us."

'If women are working from home the company gets an enormous amount. The women give a lot. There is concentrated effort, high dedication and commitment. The company has to realise there's a lot in it for them.'

ICL does not only accommodate women to keep them on, but is also interested in their career development. Ms Arnold was worried that her time away would count against her, particularly as she had also moved with her family, causing her to change her work site, but she is now Manager of Product Validation, managing 115 people.

Sue McClaren-Thomson is a Senior Manager in Sales, traditionally a male preserve. She was the first woman Sales Branch Manager. She says: 'I have worked for enlightened managers. But I always make sure I have enough experience to make it easy for them to promote me. There are women coming up behind me, but children slow them down – they go away and take time to get back.'

She has noticed an increasing number of women in management during her twenty-one years with the company: 'Men used to be the safe option. Now male managers are less and less afraid to hire and promote women.'

Although Ms McClaren-Thomson advises women to 'be over-qualified because it makes it easier to be appointed', she dropped out of her university course as an ICL-sponsored student and went to work for the company instead. Her lack of a degree has not held her back.

Ms McClaren-Thomson is a member of the Thursday Club. It started in 1985 as a group of women managers which used to meet on Thursdays. The group aims to encourage more women into management positions by those who are already there acting as role models and mentors. It also provides women managers with a regular opportunity to meet one another. At many of the Thursday Club meetings, there are guest speakers ranging from women directors of other companies and equal opportunities proponents, to experts on colour co-ordination in fashion.

All this is to be applauded. However, long hours are expected from senior managers. Ms McClaren-Thomson does a sixty-hour week in the office, with two or three hours a day travelling. She rarely works at weekends, preferring to put more hours in during the week.

However good ICL's policies are, some of the men in ICL resist change. Nevertheless, ICL undoubtedly goes further than most companies in its genuine commitment to women, both in putting their skills to good use and in making it as easy as possible for them to combine work and family.

Rank Xerox was founded some thirty years ago as an Anglo-American venture. Today the company is a leading supplier of document processing equipment in over eighty countries. Rank Xerox (UK) Ltd is the marketing and support arm of the Rank Xerox organisation in the UK. It employs some 4,500 people in over fifty locations, with the headquarters in Uxbridge, west of London. About a quarter of the staff are women working in jobs ranging from clerical assistant to senior manager.

Rank Xerox

Equal Opps Policy	✓	Crèche	✗
Equal Opps Recruitment	✓	Career Breaks	✓
Monitoring	✓	Jobshares	✓
Positive Action	✓	Flexible Hours	✓

Rank Xerox may not have been among the first companies to realise that equal opportunities make good business sense but, once committed, it is certainly taking equal opportunities seriously. It is looking at recruiting more women, particularly in male-dominated areas, promoting increasing numbers of women into management and making it easier for women to return after maternity leave.

The task is not easy. Mel Burrows, a District After-Sales Manager in Bristol, says that in the last six months she has hired five men for her team. Out of the sixty applicants not one was a woman: 'We ran a national positive action advertisement which attracted some women, but not as many as we would have hoped. We're actively requesting the guys to think about women they know who could work here – including their wives.'

Ms Burrows is used to being the only woman and says she has encountered no discrimination: 'I'm treated as one of the lads.' However, she believes that having more women in the technical areas would be good for the company: 'It would give more breadth because women tackle things in different ways. Of course, they should still be hired entirely on ability – otherwise it is not fair on them or the guys.'

Four out of ten graduates Rank Xerox takes on are women and even those not technically trained are encouraged to go into male-dominated areas. Lynn Baillie went into sales when she joined seven years ago and rose to become a Key Account Executive. When she had Francesca two years ago she began finding the work difficult: 'I came back full-time for a year but was not happy because I felt I was not seeing Francesca. I contacted a former colleague, Helen, who had not come back after having her baby because she wanted part-time and could not get it. We approached the company to do a jobshare. Personnel were good and receptive. My manager had not realised I had a problem because I was working full-time but, if I had not be allowed to jobshare, I would probably have left.

'I don't think it would have worked for everybody. It is important who you share with: I worked with Helen before and there was mutual respect. The manager liked the way we were determined that we were going to make it work. As we are in sales, we work to targets and we're doing well, which is good.

'The company has kept the experience and commitment of two people – they had about sixteen years of experience to lose. The days worked in the jobshare are very full days – you can't let your colleague down.

'For me it is wonderful. I don't feel so pressured. Previously, I was rushing to get home but now if I don't see her one evening it's no big deal.'

Ms Baillie says the Personnel Department has established a 'can do' attitude throughout the company: 'Personnel won't turn things away. They always look at any proposal to alter work patterns and if it's a good case they will support you.'

For Hilary Wilson, who is one of the few women Business Consultants in the company, the hurdle of how to deal with work and a baby has yet to be met. She is at home with 3-week-old Ross working out how she will juggle her commitments.

She says she felt she had experienced some discrimination in the length of time it took her to be promoted. She had been promised promotion for a year but it kept being put off: 'I had to put in a lot of work. I had to put in all the hours, and all the courses and all the training required, so they had no reason not to give it to me.' She was finally promoted just as she discovered she was pregnant. Her manager was reluctant to implement the rise until she returned from maternity leave, but the Personnel Department pointed out that pregnancy had nothing to do with promotion: 'They said that as far as promotion was concerned my pregnancy did not exist.'

Rank Xerox offers a range of options to women on maternity leave from a career break for up to three years to various forms of flexible working. Career breaks are available for childcare as well as for completing full-time education, political service or amateur sports, like competing in the Olympics. In order to encourage women to return to work within twenty-nine weeks of the birth, two months salary is paid on the completion of six months service. Those who return within four months of the birth also retain all the perks that go with the job, like a company car and private medical insurance.

Although Hilary Wilson feels she was held back slightly, she thinks a lot of effort was put into her career: 'They have trained me up very well and the fact that I got as far as I have is pretty good going. It's a great company to work for.'

Throughout the company the policy to encourage women into management goes to the very top. It is well known that the Managing Director wants more women managers and even a woman director. At the moment the board has one woman on it.

Ms Burrows says:'I honestly believe that they are a fair employer. Corporately, they encourage women to bring them into the business. At the top jobs become fewer and promotion prospects tighter, but I would like to move forward and the climate will not stop me, as a woman, from progressing to the top.'

Rank Xerox is still looking at new initiatives for women to encourage them to join the company and progress within it. It will take time to discover if the practice is living up to the policies, but the future looks hopeful.

MANUFACTURING

Imperial Chemical Industries (ICI) employs 54,000 people in the UK and 133,000 people worldwide, researching and manufacturing chemical and biological products. The head office is in London but it has major plants in Bracknell, Runcorn, Teeside, Alderley Edge, Fernhurst, Slough and Grangemouth. Abroad, ICI is represented in almost all European countries, the USA, Japan, the Far East, Australia and South America. About 10,000 of its employees are women (20 per cent).

Imperial Chemical Industries (ICI)

Equal Opps Policy	✓	Crèche	✓
Equal Opps Recruitment	✓	Career Breaks	✓
Monitoring	✓	Jobshares	✓
Positive Action	✓	Flexible Hours	✓

In these days when science graduates are more valuable than gold dust, ICI has realised it is not merely a matter of recruiting women chemists and biologists but also of retaining them. As well as offering good promotion prospects, the company has recently devised an imaginative maternity package.

In 1989 one-third of science graduates taken on were women: the company would like to recruit equal numbers of each sex, but women scientists are still in the minority in universities and polytechnics. This is a big change from twenty-seven years ago when Anne Ferguson, now in her late forties, joined and found herself to be one of only two women in the whole of the ICI Paints Group. She was the first woman in Dulux marketing and puts her success down to her gender: 'It's women customers who choose and buy paint. I worked out why women choose the particular paint they do and it was easy to market it.'

As Head of Group Communications, she is ICI's most senior woman and one of the most senior 400 employees worldwide: 'They've treated me terribly well. I've been very lucky and always done a job I liked. Every time I have been bored with whatever I have been doing I have moved on to something else. I have been able to combine a career with a satisfying home life without finding it difficult to achieve a balance.'

She has been head hunted often, but never seriously tempted: 'I enjoy the job, the people I work with are bright, nice and friendly, and I am well paid. I look at the other companies and mostly what they have to offer doesn't meet the range here.'

Female senior managers are not an oddity, but they are still quite rare. Carol Eastwood, who joined ICI fourteen years ago, is now in her mid-thirties, the Chief Analyst in the ICI Colours and Fine Chemicals Business: 'When I first started eight of us went on an induction course and I was the only woman. Now six of us are senior managers or senior scientists: ICI considers becoming a senior manager the major hurdle. All six of us achieved that within three years of each other and I was about in the middle. I felt quite proud because the others hadn't taken time out to have a baby.'

Dr Eastwood says there is enormous scope for achievement in the company: 'ICI is driven by opportunity and ability. If you've got ability and demonstrate it, you will get the chances. However, if you are by nature more retiring it will count against you. So, if women are less confident on average, then that will work its way through.'

Her one regret was that when she had her son, Jonathan, ICI did not operate a career break scheme. Instead she negotiated her return to work with her manager and at first this included shorter hours. Now, up to five years can be taken off for looking after children or elderly relatives by men or women; in fact fathers will be encouraged to take career breaks. ICI is one of the few companies which recognise that employees may need to take time off to care for a dependent or dying relative. Encouraging fathers to take career breaks may go some way to ensure that parents make demands at ICI rather than just mothers. Seven people had taken career breaks by the end of 1990.

An information scientist in Ms Eastwood's section worked from home for six months, deciding to delay her return to work after having a baby. ICI installed a computer in her house and Dr Eastwood says it worked well for everyone. She stresses it is important that every case is looked at individually to find the best solution.

As well as career breaks, ICI has extended its maternity leave to fifty-two weeks, with eighteen weeks paid at 90 per cent of normal salary, as opposed to the statutory six weeks. Alternatively, women may agree, with their managers, flexible working arrangements, such as part-time work, to ease their return to employment or discrete periods of time off for childcare responsibilities in the first two years. The company has declared a greater commitment to flexible working arrangements – part-time and jobshare options.

Theresa Jones is another mother who regrets the lack of choice when she gave birth to Gemma in 1986: 'I was determined to come back when I discovered I was pregnant: I had invested six years at university and five years at ICI. When Gemma was 6 weeks old, they asked me to come in and brief someone; it was so nice to feel wanted I decided I wanted to come back right away but I couldn't manage full-time. I worked out an unofficial arrangement with my manager to work one day a week in January, two in February, steadily increasing month by month until I was full-time.

'Then I discovered I was missing the baby. I asked for part-time but was told it was not possible as a member of staff and I would have to resign. I was offered part-time for a special project but would have had to have resigned from my staff position and be given a fixed-term contract. So I stayed full-time. I was a bit annoyed and felt it was a bit archaic.'

Three years later she was offered a project to lead which was too small to sustain a full-timer and gladly went part-time, which she had always wanted: 'I've now proved to myself and everyone else that I could hold down a full-time job and my career is up and running again. But it's been wonderful doing things with Gemma.

'I do think ICI has changed. When I joined there were very few women above lab grades and there are more now, as well as a lot coming in at the lower grades, although there are not many women senior managers. I am used to going to meetings and being the only woman. It's changing but it's got a long way to go.

'If women go off and have families, it puts the brakes on their career progression. They see me as not very dedicated; some managers feel I'm just treading water.'

ICI is not only worried about keeping mothers on but also about how it treats women generally. A shift in management perception is being encouraged so that line managers from each ICI business review the current recruitment, turnover and career development of women, and set themselves managerial objectives for improvement in their area. A regular internal monitoring system to assess progress is also being set in place.

Dr Eastwood says that the biggest change to ICI may come from the women they are hiring: 'They are far more demanding and more assured. They can make demands about the kind of support they expect, and on their career development. When I joined in the seventies I felt lucky to get any job, now young people are far more confident. The women coming in expect nothing short of equality: they've never experienced anything else. They are a powerful force for change.'

Mars Confectionery is part of Mars Incorporated, a privately owned multi-national corporation. It makes the eponymous Mars bar and a range of other confectionery snacks and is based in Slough. The corporation also makes and markets pet food and pet care products, main meal foods, electronics, beverage vending machines and information management services.

Mars

Equal Opps Policy	✓	Crèche	✓
Equal Opps Recruitment	✓	Career Breaks	✓
Monitoring	✓	Jobshares	✗
Positive Action	✓	Flexible Hours	✓

Mars has always prided itself on being one of the best employers in the UK. The corporation's philosophy is based on the premise that if 'associates', as staff are called, are treated as individuals, individual contribution is greater, which directly benefits the company. It is a highly paid egalitarian company where not even the Managing Director has a private office - his desk is part of the open plan environment. Everyone has to clock on and earns a 10 per cent daily bonus for punctuality.

Mars is a company which takes the development of the individual seriously, providing training in technical and interpersonal skills to ensure that the growth of the associate will benefit the company. Yet, in the midst of all this, the company recognised that not enough women were winning through into management. Valerie Ann Waters, in charge of Affirmative Action, put it in Mars-speak: 'We're the best people in our business, yet we haven't got our share of the female talent.'

In April 1989, Ms Waters was given the task of developing an action programme for increasing the number of women in management. In January 1990, the policy was implemented. It includes:

■ A maternity package giving up to forty weeks off, with six months on 90 per cent pay. At the end of maternity leave, there is the option of up to six months part-time on coming back, or up to five years off for a career break.

■ Places in the nearby crèche

■ Overhauling recruitment procedures, including targeted advertising

■ Targets for the number of women managers

■ The returners support network, which includes a workshop.

What is interesting about Mars' approach is that it is driven as much by the special talents women are seen to have as by a general desire not to waste the potential of the workforce. The General Manager and many senior men want to increase the number of women in management because they believe that with sufficient numbers to make an impact, women will alter the company's style for the better. They feel that a more intuitive approach will add something to the decision-making process.

A survey done by the company showed that most women in management positions were young with no children: almost 66 per cent were under 30, while 10 per cent had school-age children and a further 7 per cent were pregnant. The company has recently targeted women returners to improve the balance of the workforce. A 'Welcome Back' advertisement has been placed and a *Returning To Work* information booklet produced. These have generated a lot of inquiries but no successful candidates as yet.

If Pat Doble is anything to go by, women returners are treated well. She stopped working for nine years to bring up her children before applying for a market research job at Mars. During the interview the issue of her children was raised, but she says the prevailing attitude was that in applying for the job she had decided to return to work and it was not up to the company to question whether she could cope. She is now one of the most senior women in the company.

Mars realised the benefit of innovative steps in 1988 when it ran a recruitment advertisement in the *Sunday Times* asking for applications from women engineers. Normal advertisements attracted about 150 replies, of which some fifteen were from women. This one led to 560 applicants, two-thirds of whom were women. Not only was there a massive response from women, but more men replied than had ever previously to an advertisement aimed at both sexes.

Jenny Reynolds, a Shift Manager in charge of production, was one of the successful applicants to respond to that advertisement. A graduate, she was in the marketing department of another manufacturing company. She wanted to get out of marketing but had not thought of getting involved in the production process until she saw the advertisement. She will now probably seek to broaden her experience in the company but says her production line experience has been fascinating. Interestingly, she was worried about the introduction of targeted percentages for women in her male dominated area because of the way she felt she would be treated if her male colleagues suspected reverse discrimination. In fact, Mars has no intention of dropping the quality of its recruits, and applies the same calibre standards for men and women. Even the advertisement for women engineers resulted in equal numbers of women and men being recruited. The concern about women possibly being accorded special privileges appears to be widespread among women in the company.

Ms Waters says the benefits from the new maternity package of retaining women at all levels in the business are beginning to show. In customer services, during 1990, six of the staff, one-fifth of the department, became pregnant. Five of these returned from maternity leave, initially to various patterns of part-time work, from ten to thirty hours a week. All five are now back full-time. To deal with these work patterns, there was increased co-operation, communication and understanding within the department. Part-time work is still only available on an extremely limited basis, but patterns of working is an area which is currently being re-examined.

The Learning and Development Manager, Bernadette Fisher, who has a 2-year-old boy gave the reason why so many people enjoy working for Mars: 'The people are very stimulating. If you think you're good at something, come to Mars and you'll find someone better. It's like playing tennis, it pulls your game up.'

*Smith's manufacture far more than the crisps which give the
company its name. The products include: Quavers, the UK's
first savoury snack launched in 1968; Planters, the biggest
selling nuts in the world; and Monster Munch and Savoury
Moments. The company also produces 'own label' brands for
Marks & Spencer, Sainsbury's and Tesco. Smiths is owned by
the American food giant Pepsico and has its headquarters in
Reading, although there are factories throughout the country.
It employs 3,365 people, 1,375 of whom are women.*

Smith's

Equal Opps Policy	✓	Crèche	✗
Equal Opps Recruitment	✓	Career Breaks	✗
Monitoring	✗	Jobshares	✓
Positive Action	✗	Flexible Hours	✓

Smith's is one of the few manufacturing companies which is
seriously looking at equal opportunities and beginning to take
action. It has a good record on promoting women: the thirty
women in management represent over 12 per cent of the total,
there are six women in senior management and the first woman
director was appointed in 1990. Some of those women have
children and for the most part they are expected to treat their
children like most working fathers do: firmly coming second to the
job. However, there are signs of change.

Sarah Newman is a Marketing Manager with two children, a 3
year old and 1 year old. She was asked to apply for the job while
she was with a rival manufacturer and has been with Smith's for
six months: 'They knew I had children. I made sure they knew.
I wanted a company which could accommodate the occasional
crisis. I've been lucky not to have one.

'My husband and I see childcare as a joint responsibility. We
have a full-time nanny who does work long hours. I quite often take

work home with me so I can see the children. If I have a sick child I tend to leave earlier. It is absolutely physically exhausting, especially if I'm up in the night.'

Personnel Manager Christine MacNevin has the same difficulties: 'The greatest problem about working with young children is juggling hours. People do a very long day. Lots of jobs have to be done after hours. I find it very difficult; in order to get work done I take it home.

'Smith's hasn't got an overall attitude about doing anything in particular. The attitude of the company depends on the individual person you report to. It encourages women to return, but there is a long way to go in making it easier for women to come back. In my case, I was allowed to come back two days a week at the beginning, but I work on projects and the projects could wait until I got back. It depends on the job and the job requirement.'

One of the senior managers is about to leave to have her second baby. In her case, Smith's will provide home facilities such as a fax and a terminal to enable her to maintain close contact with the office. She will also be encouraged to work as she wants while she is on maternity leave.

Ms MacNevin says: 'We are looking at jobsharing, but not in any co-ordinated way, and not in management. In Personnel, we are trying to set an example: if I wanted to find another person and thought it would work they would give it a go.

'We are starting to send people who have been on maternity leave, or are going on it, to Working Mothers' Association workshops, so they will be able to know what they are coming back to. We are also reconsidering our maternity leave policy so that we are competitive in the market place. We're making moves but not putting massive resources into it. We have to put some money into it, but it is limited.'

The company is moving to a different part of Reading and a crèche is being considered at the new headquarters.

Smith's runs Women's Development courses for women at junior management and supervisory level with an opportunity to develop. The contents of the course include assertiveness training, talks from women managers, presentation skills and leadership skills. Julie Ballard, the Employee Relations Manager, ran the

SMITH'S   **151**

courses last year and says she received very good feedback: 'They had all gone away from the course with action plans, and at the follow-up meeting six months later, they had all achieved or progressed towards the achievement of their objectives.'

The ability of many of the women in the company is recognised. Mrs Newman stresses that promotion is absolutely on merit, although she believes that having children has held her career back: 'With twelve years experience in marketing management I could have expected to be a director by now. However, as a company it is totally accepting about what comes with senior females. The current Managing Director and Marketing Director are open minded about it and I'm sure would not put forward my personal position as a barrier to promotion.'

Sue Neville Weaver is the Financial Controller and has been with the company six years. She joined as Commercial Accountant and was steadily promoted to reach her position. She says Smith's promote on merit: 'I have had to prove myself, but if you really prove yourself to be better you will get recognition. You have to be prepared to work all hours including weekends.'

She is determined that her next step will be up to Director of Finance and does not envisage her gender getting in the way of that promotion.

Smith's does not compare well with many of the companies in the other sectors, but Julie Ballard says: 'Smith's is only a medium sized company in a very competitive and low margin business, therefore it does not have the funds, like the finance sector and oil companies, to afford the things it would like to provide like maternity leave on full pay or a subsidised crèche. However, we do recognise the need to recruit, retain and develop more women in order to meet the business needs of the future: our aim is to attract more women and become the "employer of choice". During the next few years we shall be re-launching our equal opportunities policy and developing strategies to achieve this.'

Christine MacNevin sums up Smith's: 'It is a company which realises things have to be done. It is now making moves and will continue to gear itself up for greater moves in the next couple of years.'

MEDIA

*The BBC has television and radio centres throughout
England, Scotland, Wales and Northern Ireland. It
encompasses a range of disciplines: engineer, film-maker,
journalist and production assistant to name a few. Almost
12,000 of the 28,000 employees are women.*

BBC

Equal Opps Policy	✓	Crèche	✓
Equal Opps Recruitment	✓	Career Breaks	✓
Monitoring	✓	Jobshares	✓
Positive Action	✓	Flexible Hours	✓

The BBC offers enormous scope to its staff due to its size and its
varied areas of programming in both radio and television.
However, there is almost a gender demarcation of jobs, with most
women in the lower paid, lower status, supportive roles. Wardrobe,
make-up and production assistant are still seen to be very much
women's tasks, whilst men tend to be sound and camera operators.
Women are breaking into the men's areas, but there are still
women's ghettos at the BBC.

The Corporate Equal Opportunities Department, set up in 1986,
has gone some way towards improving the situation. One positive
action course a year gives women in administration access to the
technical side of broadcasting: more than half the graduates on
these courses are now doing technical or production jobs.

Since 1986 about 100 women a year have been on women-only
courses for managers. In 1989, a survey showed that half of the
women who replied had been promoted. There is a drive for

managers to make sure that they send their women staff with
potential on courses in the same way as they send their men with
potential on courses. As a result, the percentage of women on
management development courses has increased to 50 per cent.

Cherry Erlich, who was the first Head of the Equal
Opportunities Department, says: 'Senior management are
actively and positively committed to pursue and monitor the
BBC's equal opportunities policies. This has lead to significant
changes in the gender profile in management and production
areas. For example, it is a big increase to go from fifty-seven to
1,765 women at Head of Department level. It represents nearly
25 per cent of all posts at this level.'

Di Mansfield is an Assistant Producer on the BBC2 television
arts programme *Arena*; she occasionally directs programmes. She
started in 1971 as a Production Assistant and remembers that in
those days PAs were called 'sweetie girls'. Most PAs were in the
job for life and it was rare for them to be promoted. In spite of
the recent changes she could not say that there is real
equality:'I'm not that ambitious, I'm not that pushy, so I can't
blame them for holding my career back, but the boys do get the
jobs more than the girls.

'In the last five years the intake of women researchers is much,
much higher. Therefore women are more likely to go on to be
producers and directors: there are still relatively few of those in
music and arts.

'The BBC has got better. Anything that goes on by way of
sexism is subtle. But on *Arena* male graduates come in and
somehow just get on quicker - it just seems to be easier for men.
Do they inspire more confidence? Or are they more confident?'

Sheryl Crown, in her mid thirties, is a Script Editor in the
Television Drama Department. She finds that how well women are
treated depends on their rank and status: 'Secretaries are very
much secretaries, but women in more senior positions are treated
well. There are an awful lot of women in the Drama Department,
women producers old and young, but fewer women directors.
Perhaps this is because producing uses traditional female skills.'

Ms Crown is on an annual contract, which has automatically
been renewed since she started there in early 1989. This is a

growing practice in the BBC, which while it may get rid of any
complacency certainly does not allow for a sense of security. She
has no children yet, but is not ruling babies out of her career plan.
However, she thinks the job would be very difficult with young
children: 'The job varies but it is never easy. I am expected to work
long and irregular hours when necessary.' The only woman with
young children in her department – her immediate boss – has a
husband who stays at home.

The problem of irregular hours is endemic in the BBC, partly
because of scheduling – programmes go out twenty-four hours a
day – and partly because of the compelling nature of the job. There
is also an element of tradition in working long hours which is
literally intended to sort out the men from the boys, and to prove
one's single-minded dedication to the corporation.

Fiona Chesterton, in her late thirties, was on the television
current affairs programme *60 Minutes* when she first got
pregnant and the programme was axed while she was on
maternity leave in 1984. She went on to the local television news
programme, *London Plus*: 'They were very supportive to me
coming back part-time and staying on staff, but the Personnel
Department did not want my arrangement to be well known. I was
on thirty hours instead of forty-two hours, getting three-quarters
pay.'

When Ms Chesterton went for a promotion, to a job she had been
doing unofficially for years, she was told she would not get it
because she was part-time. A new Department Director then told
her she was not committed to the BBC because she was working
part-time. She went off to have her second baby unsure of what
she was returning to. During her maternity leave John Birt
arrived at the BBC and there was a complete upheaval: 'The South
East was hived off away from News and Current Affairs television
and I was offered a senior producer job while on maternity leave.
Within two hours of coming back I was offered the job of Editor
of the programme. I made it clear I couldn't work the hours of my
predecessor – twelve hours a day.

'My immediate boss is very supportive but there is no question
it's a full-time job. I take my elder daughter, Sarah, to school every
morning so I don't get in till 9.45 or 10 a.m. I delegate to the senior

producers the job of getting the show on the road – they can always phone me at home. I know there are lots of jobs where that would be unacceptable. I take quite a few Friday mornings off, as it's a quiet day, tending to get in at lunchtime – except the day of the IRA bombing of the marines at Deal, when my bleep went off in Sainsbury's.'

Ms Chesterton has benefited from the new approach to women in the BBC. Sarah has even been to the Elstree holiday playscheme, which Fiona recommends. However, there is a price for the time she gives to her children: 'If I were to go for promotion, I know there would be no truck with the "I want to take my daughter to school". I haven't gone for quite a few jobs because of the hours I would have to work.

'I get the feeling the South East actually value me. Quite a few women in bigger departments feel they can just be replaced. Things have changed enormously.'

Ms Chesterton has not taken advantage of either the BBC's new career break or jobsharing schemes. While there are nothing like enough crèche places to meet the needs of employees, more and more BBC nurseries are opening throughout the UK.

Unfortunately, for every positive story about the BBC there are tales of appalling discrimination, in favour of young men, for example, as compared with pregnant or part-time women. Little is said because, although the policy is to monitor appointments, so much promotion is about 'faces fitting' that a fuss only ensures an end to any opportunities for promotion. As Ms Chesterton says: 'I think it depends where you are at any particular time. Although there are equal opportunities guidelines and principles, it depends where you are as to how much notice is taken of them.'

The BBC was traditionally a place where women began as secretaries and worked their way up. This has changed dramatically over the years; as women's confidence and expectations have increased, so many go in as journalists, film-makers or whatever career paths they intend to follow. However, there are still opportunities for secretaries to progress, particularly in radio.

Overall the BBC is trying hard and the policies, backed from the very top, prove that the will to encourage women to achieve their full potential does exist. However, breaking down the prejudices of the producers and editors of individual programmes will be considerably more difficult.

Channel Four commissions and transmits the programmes it shows but it does not itself make any programmes apart from Right to Reply, *which allows viewers to answer back. The programmes are commissioned from independent production companies or bought in from other television companies in this country and abroad. The channel is part of the independent television sector operating in England, Scotland and Northern Ireland – there is a separate service in Wales: S4C. The headquarters are in London's chic Charlotte Street. Over half of the 394 employees are women who do a vast array of jobs from clerical work to commissioning programmes.*

Channel Four

Equal Opps Policy	✓	Crèche	✗
Equal Opps Recruitment	✓	Career Breaks	✗
Monitoring	✓	Jobshares	✓
Positive Action	✗	Flexible Hours	✓

Women certainly seem to enjoy working for Channel Four. There are progressive policies and there seems to be a friendliness and attention to individual needs.

Bernadette O'Farrell, an Assistant Commissioning Editor for Documentaries, said: 'It's a very supportive place to work, if something goes wrong people support you rather than blame you. It's quite small, so I know everyone. It's just a nice place to work and that's why people stay.'

Channel Four began on a cloud of high expectations – the station which would provide answers to everybody's gripes. Susan Dunkley, who is now the Promotions Officer, was so determined to work for the channel at the age of 37 that she went back to being a secretary to get a job there. It did not take her long to start taking on more responsibility and she has no regrets: 'It's chaotic, but every day it's different. It's very exciting, and non-stop. You have got to be the sort of person who likes hopping from one crisis to another. The only problem is that I have to be careful not to get so involved – I forget everything else.'

She works long hours – 8.45 a.m. to 7 p.m. with the odd weekend thrown in. It is typical of the long hours culture at the channel. Bernadette O'Farrell starts at 9.30 a.m. and rarely finishes before 8 at night. She also travels a lot: 'It does intrude into my private life. I don't mind but I might in future. When I first started, I used to work weekends, but I was getting very tired. Now I don't, in order to do the work properly.'

Caroline Thomson, who was the Commissioning Editor for Finance, Industry and Science, has now been promoted to Head of Corporate Affairs. She has a 2-year-old son, Andrew, and invariably leaves at 6 p.m. She realises she is privileged, but had to run the gauntlet on her third day back from maternity leave when she was in a meeting with the Head of Channel Four, Michael Grade: 'I stood up, feeling very shy and said I have got to go home now and feed the baby. I was breastfeeding and there was no option. That's the way I have worked since: I've taken work home and sometimes if there's a crisis I come back to work again after Andrew is in bed.

'I have been surprised at how relieved the men are. I was in a meeting once trying to sort out a very complicated programme about Cecil Parkinson. At 6 I said I had to go but offered to come back again. The Controller of Factual Programmes, John Willis, said that actually he had a parents' evening at school and the reporter, Christo Hird, had a child with a bad cold who he wanted to put to bed. I had allowed both of them to do what they really wanted to do.'

Ms Thomson says she has found working at the channel a joy since the birth of Andrew: 'It's the best of all possible worlds. For the first six or eight months, when the baby was not sleeping through the night, I would be in bed by 10 p.m. three nights a week. Now he's 2 I do miss not being at home more. I have occasionally brought Andrew into the office and everyone has been wonderful about that. The problem with going home at 6 is that in order to get the work done I cram everything in and there is no time to relax at work: no lunches or drinks or gossip. I have found it easier than I thought it would be but even so there is still a thin line between coping marvellously and complete chaos.'

In January 1991 the channel decided to radically improve the provisions for mothers. All working mothers with children under the age of 14 receive £100 per month towards the cost of childcare, and it is lobbying the government to allow tax relief on all childcare expenses. Mothers will have up to a week's compassionate leave to help deal with emergencies. Paid maternity leave for women who have worked at Channel Four for over eighteen months will be increased from three to four months, and women outside the qualifying period will receive a month's paid leave. All vacancies will be assessed as possible jobshare posts.

All three women point to the most senior female executive in Channel Four, Director of Programmes Liz Forgan, as having a decisive influence for the better. Ms Thomson says that when she was pregnant and working on a particularly sensitive programme with legal problems, she was making herself ill – working weekends as well as evenings: 'Liz just told me to go home and told me not to come back until I was absolutely fine. She was not at all grudging, she cared about my health and the baby. She was really fantastic.'

Bernadette O'Farrell says it makes a tremendous difference having equal amounts of female and male commissioning editors around the boardroom table in meetings. She also points to two secretaries who have been promoted to assistant editors during the two and a half years she has been with the channel as evidence that it is not only senior women who are treated well.

The main complaint is the tiny budgets and low staffing. What requires two people in the BBC or ITV only has one member of staff at Channel Four, and the budgets can be a tenth of those of their rivals. However, even this is treated more as a challenge than a problem.

Women are obviously well treated, with self defence courses for women and the first jobshare being the latest examples of how the channel is tackling individual needs. However, the great irony is that the effect of the channel on the wider industry is far from progressive for women. Independent production companies have been formed based on the channel's commissions which give no security to their staff; few contracts are even for a year. This practice has spread throughout the industry, which means there are no maternity provisions. People are hired to make a programme or series of programmes, there is little slack and working evenings and weekends becomes the norm. There is little action on equal opportunities in the independent sector.

This said, Channel Four obviously does take its obligations to its own direct employees seriously.

*London Weekend Television is the independent television
station which serves the London area from Friday evening
until Monday morning. Many of its programmes are screened
nationally. LWT produces drama, documentaries, current
affairs programmes, games shows and chat shows. Its offices
are on London's South Bank. It employs 1,214 people, of
which 410 are women (35 per cent of the workforce).*

London Weekend Television

Equal Opps Policy	✓	Crèche	✓
Equal Opps Recruitment	✓	Career Breaks	✗
Monitoring	✓	Jobshares	✗
Positive Action	✓	Flexible Hours	✓

London Weekend Television has been in the forefront of pushing
for equal opportunities for women. The company took places in the
nearby Kingsway crèche, in London's Holborn, when it first
opened in 1977 and now flexible working hours can be negotiated
on return from maternity leave. Targets have been set for women
and ethnic minorities up to the year 2000, so that LWT can 'employ
a workforce which reflects the LWT area population at all levels
of the organisation'.

Kate Hynes, who as the Controller of Production Planning is one
of the two most senior women at LWT, used the crèche from its
first day for her son, Llewelyn, and her two other children also
spent several years there. Ms Hynes says the crèche made the
whole difference to her ability to work as previously she had been
leaving LWT at 4.30 p.m. to pick up Llewelyn from a childminder.
She had not intended to return to work but her husband's business
collapsed and she was forced to: 'The second time I had no doubts
about coming back. I knew the nursery was there, which made a
lot of difference.'

Christine Cant, a make-up supervisor with a young baby, cannot use the crèche because her hours are so irregular. Nor is it of much use to those commuting from outside London. Personnel staff at LWT are aware that it is far from a universal answer to their employees' childcare problems.

There is a financial incentive for women to return from maternity leave at LWT: this is a lump sum payment of six weeks pay on return to work which is refundable if the woman leaves within six months. Over 70 per cent of women do return to work. When women come back from maternity leave they can negotiate reduced hours with their manager, if this is considered feasible. This has been made a great deal easier by an edict from Managing Director Greg Dyke stating that if any woman is refused shorter hours the reason must be given to him in writing.

Helen Auty, Training and Equal Opportunities Adviser and a parent herself, says Mr Dyke's public backing of equal opportunity policies has given them enormous weight. While LWT still is very much a feudal kingdom with little fiefdoms, individual managers are aware that their actions are being scrutinised. Ms Hynes said: 'He put his enormous power behind the Equal Opportunities Committee, so research has been done and money put into it. He's given powerful backing to the whole movement.'

LWT has now introduced targeting for recruitment. At the moment, 35 per cent of the workforce are women, but the aim is to increase that figure to 40 per cent by 1992 and to a minimum of 43 per cent by the year 2000. Already, half of the junior management is female and 21 per cent of controllers and heads of departments. Ms Hynes remembers when the only female controller was the Company Secretary. When she was made Head of Department, it never occurred to her that she would ever be promoted to Controller because she was a woman and 'it used to be thought women weren't the stuff Controllers were made of'.

Deborah Arnott is a Producer/Director on the *London Programme* and has both her children in the crèche. She was one of the founders of the Equal Opportunities Committee which was created after her report back from a *European Women in Television* conference. She enjoys her work and while she has some criticisms of LWT's practice she agrees that they are better than a lot of other companies. Now in her thirties, she started as a researcher seven years ago and says: 'They are very good at promoting. In many other television companies women researchers never move.'

She feels the efforts of the Personnel Department have paid off: 'They try to foster the small company image. The Director of Personnel genuinely wants people to be happy here and cares about people. After the Clapham rail disaster, he went round checking who was missing and whether anybody had been on the train. When a secretary was murdered on her way home he understood how threatened many of the women here felt, while some of my male colleagues were totally unsympathetic. There is a traditional, paternalistic attitude to employees – in a nice way. It has always seemed like a family company – rather insular. They tend to promote from within which is good for women because men don't get pulled in above you.

'To get ahead here you need a sponsor and for women that sponsor is almost always going to be a man.'

In the Make-up Department, of course, it is all women. Make-up is all too often seen as just powdering noses. Christine Cant considers herself, quite rightly, as creative as anybody in the company: she won a BAFTA (British Academy of Film & Television Arts) award in 1988. She came from the BBC and says: 'LWT is a fabulous company to work for. They take care of you and it's good and interesting work.'

She decided not to go part-time when she returned from having her son because: 'You end up doing all the crummy shows. I do the job so I can work on dramas and comedy.' She is now at the top of her scale and for the moment is happy to stay there while her son, Joe, grows up, but eventually she hopes to move to yet more demanding work.

The Personnel Department is committed to keeping talented women like Ms Cant in the company and ensuring they continue to progress.

Television is a competitive business needing highly skilled people to produce high quality programmes so it makes sense to treat employees well, in the way LWT does. On the other hand, people are desperate to get into the business and there is always new talent knocking on the door. So it is heartening to see that

LWT does far more than the bare minimum for its women employees and has a genuine commitment to equal opportunities.

*Research & Development Services is a market research and
management consultancy that started in 1984. It deals in new
product development research, strategic development and
advertising, both creative and strategy research, mainly in the
food, drink, leisure and finance industries. It is based in
north London. RDS employs twenty-six people, twenty-one of
whom are women; over half of the employees are executive
researchers.*

Research & Development Services (RDS)

Equal Opps Policy	✗	Crèche	✓
Equal Opps Recruitment	✗	Career Breaks	✗
Monitoring	✓	Jobshares	✗
Positive Action	✗	Flexible Hours	✓

RDS is much better in practice towards its women employees than
the above table would indicate. The company's small size means
that its policies are individually tailored, rather than formal,
which is why there is not an equal opportunities policy.

RDS is an excellent example of what a small company can
achieve. Some of the employees say it is like being part of a family
and many of the decisions derive from the best elements of a
paternalistic/maternalistic philosophy. When the three partners –
two males and one female – who started the company became
parents, they experienced the challenges of combining parenthood
and a career, and began to consider how these stresses would
affect the staff. Wendy Mitchell is one of the directors and now
has two children herself: 'We thought long and hard about the
staff. We had all options open to us because we are reasonably well
off, but what about the parents on lower incomes? Originally we
set up the nursery to offer good childcare facilities on the premises
and have since benefited from good PR for both the recruitment
and retention of staff.

'If you look at it as a relative cost, it is commercially viable, because there are huge hidden costs in recruitment and retraining. It has paid dividends.'

Originally they had a nursery on the premises, however Ms Mitchell notes that not only did it begin to outgrow itself but also it only provided help for those who lived close to work. They now buy places in a Susan Hay Nursery nearby and are also prepared to buy places in other nurseries in residential areas, or subsidise childminders and nannies.

There is some regret about the loss of the nursery: 'When the nursery was on our premises all staff, not just the parents, would call in to see the children for a few minutes. It's an excellent way to relieve stress during the course of a hard day.'

Liz Phippen, a Qualitative Market Research Executive, joined the company after her son, Benjamin, was born in 1988. While she was on maternity leave from her previous job she looked around for a change: 'I was considering a number of companies, but this was much the best. There was one which was much more convenient because it was near where I live in south-west London, but the whole attitude to childcare and working mums was one of the main reasons I chose RDS. The nursery said a lot about the company's attitudes, even though I did not intend to use it myself.'

If fact, she did find the nursery the best childcare option for Benjamin. However, now Ms Phippen is again on maternity leave as she is about to have another child, and she intends to have a nanny at home, rather than take two children across London.

Ms Phippen joined as a part-timer and has never had any problems: 'They are very, very understanding. Not just those involved, but the company as a whole. In practical terms, they are flexible when necessary – there's an assumption that both sides will sort any problem out. The attitude is one of understanding which really works.'

Wendy Mitchell stresses that it works for everybody: 'We get a great deal from our part-timers, such a lot of commitment from them. They work well and do a good job. They have to organise their time well, so they are naturally very efficient.

'However, we are very sensitive about the balance within our staffing, and we do not wish to tip too much towards part-time work.'

Work is organised in research teams and RDS is careful about structuring the teams to make sure that there is a fair proportion of full and part-time workers in each one.

RDS is not only good for working parents. Ms Mitchell says there is a 'commitment to allowing personal growth and career development, and supporting staff to further their careers for the good of the individual as well as the company'. Claire Littlewood is a Qualitative Researcher, in her mid twenties, who came in on a graduate traineeship. She has been working there four years and has made good progress. She says there are plenty of opportunities in the company: 'There is no clear career ladder but there are chances to promote yourself. They recognise us all – it's a small company and we are treated as individuals. They make every effort to ensure that career ambitions are met within the company.'

The company's stated promotion policy is 'to encourage the personal growth and development of all employees as the success of a company depends on the success and job satisfaction of the staff within that company'. It seems to work remarkably well.

Ms Littlewood is also pleased about the attitude to children because 'you see yourself as being perhaps in that situation someday', and likes the company because of the 'overall encouraging and supportive attitude'.

Ms Mitchell stresses RDS is a profitable concern although its policy of giving some of those profits to charity demonstrates its altruistic side, and treating staff properly is part of being a successful company: 'It is not just the nursery *per se*, but the whole attitude to working mothers – like flexible hours and part-time working. We think these policies are working.'

These policies certainly seem to lead to an extraordinarily happy working environment. Ms Littlewood summed it up: 'Everything is done to make you feel comfortable. It's a lovely place to work. I can't criticise it at all. They don't just pay lip service to the team work idea, we are a bit of a family.'

Thames Television is the largest ITV company. It serves London and the south-east from Monday to Friday. It produces local news, current affairs, children's programmes, drama, documentaries, light entertainment and features programmes, many of which are transmitted throughout the independent region. However, the company has lost its franchise and will not have this role from 1993. In addition to Thames Television's creative and technical programme production staff, the company has an air-time sales force and an international programme sales company, Thames Television International. Thames Television has studios at both its centres, at Euston in central London, and Teddington in the south-west of the capital. It employs 1,881 people, 690 of whom are women.

Thames Television

Equal Opps Policy	✓	Crèche	✓
Equal Opps Recruitment	✓	Career Breaks	✗
Monitoring	✓	Jobshares	✓
Positive Action	✓	Flexible Hours	✓

In 1980, Thames participated in a study conducted by a lawyer, Sadie Robarts, under the auspices of the Equal Opportunities Commission and the National Council for Civil Liberties, to look at equal opportunities in the company, discover what was wrong and suggest improvements. The report, published in 1981, pulled no punches. It showed that on the technical side there were women's ghettos, such as make-up and wardrobe, which were low status and badly paid jobs, whereas the men's enclaves, made up of camera operators and engineers, were high in both status and pay. Overall, women were in the bottom ranks of the company, while most middle and senior management posts were held by men. Thames responded by appointing a board member to take responsibility for developing the positive action policy and created a post for an equal opportunities manager to try to identify the barriers faced by women in the organisation.

Over ten years later, the present Equal Opportunities Advisor, Pat Corcoran, feels the company might finally be getting it right, but she is not complacent: 'Trying hard is not good enough. We've been at it for too long, so we need to be succeeding and that's why the company is continuing to take steps. Thirty-eight per cent of Thames middle management are women and we have 14 per cent women in senior management and we are actively trying to improve that.'

One of those few senior women managers, Sandra Hepburn, who is Head of Production and Location Services, has equally high standards: 'I would not say they have got a lot better. However, there is more of an awareness which has helped women to progress.' Ms Hepburn served on the Equal Opportunities Commission for four years, between 1978 and 1982, and therefore had a heightened awareness of the problems throughout the industry at the time when Thames first began to acknowledge the need to address equal opportunities.

One benefit from the equal opportunities policy is the places at a crèche in Kingsway, near the Euston headquarters, and for some who cannot use it there is financial help. Victoria Morgan Bellamy is in this latter category. She is a Stills Assistant on *Thames News* and was offered a place in the crèche when Rosie was born: 'I wanted to use it because I looked round it and it's fabulous. But I work 8.15 a.m. to 7 p.m. and the crèche is open from 8.30 to 6.' Instead she applied for child allowance from Thames. She receives £77 a month towards the cost of a registered childminder or qualified nanny. Ms Morgan Bellamy no longer works on Fridays, which was a half day on overtime; she feels the loss of that money badly, and needs the allowance: 'I have to lose the overtime as otherwise I would never see the baby. I have to work. I have no choice. If I had a choice I wouldn't work such long hours.'

Mary McNally, who is Head of Features, says that while places at the Kingsway crèche are good, thought should be given to an in-house crèche, although in the current economic climate it is hard to see progress being made in the immediate future.

She says Thames does many good things and for a commercial company: 'It does care about its staff. It's soft at the core.' The biggest change she has noticed in her twenty years with the company are 'the video editors and camera operators who were just serried ranks of men when I came here. Now there are growing numbers of women in these jobs.'

Thames has a positive commitment to technical training for women, and there is positive commitment for women going into non-traditional areas. Thames is running an electronic maintenance course for women, aimed at A level school leavers taking their Higher National Certificate. Pat Corcoran says there are lots of young women out there with the educational background to pursue technical careers, but they find if difficult to gain experience and be accepted as realistic job applicants: 'Those that were interviewed said they were working in shops or elsewhere because they could not get interviews for engineering jobs. We are trying to break the cycle of "no experience, no job".'

After the Robarts report Thames immediately tried to recruit women in non-traditional areas. Sandra Hepburn believes this initiative backfired because there were many instances of only one woman in a section who would find herself isolated. Now the procedure has been better thought through.

Television franchises are only given to companies for a limited number of years, and the government's decision to put them up for auction to the highest bidder rather than decide on the programming ability of the competing companies, has meant insecurity. This, combined with the fall in advertising revenue, means that there is 'redundancy management' and it is a difficult time to be innovative. Ms Hepburn, like Ms Corcoran, thinks that the next goal should be management: 'There is a tendency towards female invisibility in senior management and on the board. As long as we are not there, women's potential will not be maximised. There is nothing like the critical mass of senior women in the organisation.'

Ms McNally goes further. She says there is no negative discrimination but 'it's hard for men to choose women for senior jobs in any company. It's not part of the tradition. It goes against their thinking.

'There should be more women on the board. That is an indicator of where the power is. There is only one woman – though she is very good on equal opportunities.'

Ms Hepburn says women are part of their own problem: many of them do not want to go into senior management: 'They get bored with male power games and prefer to get on and do it themselves, outside a corporate power structure. In the early eighties, when Channel Four started up, a lot of women producers who could have gone on to management decided to do their own thing and get out.'

Thames is an organisation that is not afraid of looking at itself critically. The appendix of the booklet produced by them, *Equal Opportunities in Employment*, gives a sex analysis of the organisation by job category. The results are depressing, because most of the high-earning and high-status jobs are still occupied by men, but they are probably as good, if not better, than most television companies. Seventy-eight per cent of women who have taken maternity leave in the last two years have returned to work. While the staff feel free to criticise Thames, they stay because they like it. Mary McNally says: 'I have been very happy here, that's why I'm still here. I have certainly been able to do all the programmes I want to.'

Yorkshire Television is the independent television company serving the county. It is based in Leeds. As well as producing local programmes, it makes Emmerdale Farm *in the Drama Department and from the Documentary Department comes both* First Tuesday *and* Jimmy's. *It employs almost 1,200 people, almost 400 of them are women; it has a growing number of contract staff.*

Yorkshire Television

Equal Opps Policy	✓	Crèche	✗
Equal Opps Recruitment	✓	Career Breaks	✗
Monitoring	✓	Jobshares	✓
Positive Action	✗	Flexible Hours	✓

Yorkshire Television is included in this book not because of its existing equal opportunities achievements, but because it has begun to take action over the last two years and is to be commended for this. The company does not bear comparison with the London independent television companies or the BBC, and has ignored calls from the unions over the last decade to set up an equal opportunities committee. Finally, however, the initiative has come from management, and all areas of equal opportunities for race, disability, gender and sexual harassment are under serious review by an equal opportunities committee comprising representatives of both the unions and the staff.

Policies on jobshares, career breaks, flexible hours and childcare provision are all being looked at, as well as a detailed recruitment policy. However, Judith Weymont, a Senior Researcher in the Documentaries Department, is rather sceptical about this process: 'I think two of the factors leading to the setting up of the committee were the franchise bid and the creation of the Single European Market.'

She is one of the women who pushed for the setting-up of the committee and she now sits on it: 'All the issues were brainstormed and the level of debate did not take into account the arguments and achievements of the last decade. It was a bit like trying to reinvent the wheel, but better than nothing. I think as a result, more Black people will be recruited, but in terms of promoting women or getting them into technical areas it remains to be seen whether anything is going to change radically. We have a lot of ground to catch up on but hiring a person to deal specifically with equal opportunities does not seem to be seen as a priority.'

In her ten years with Yorkshire, the station has, however, changed: 'When I came almost every job apart from researchers was a woman's job or a man's job. Now women are becoming producers in equal numbers to men and there are more women directors. There is now a woman Studio Camera Operator and a female Studio Sound Person, but there is a lot more to be done to break down the gender barriers.'

Certainly, before the inception of the Equal Opportunities Committee some women were already rising high. Sue Slee, who came in as a secretary ten years ago, is now the Manager of Programme Services: 'I expected always to be a secretary, but I was in the right place at the right time when they were looking for an Assistant Manager. Once I was in that position I started taking over. My major advantage was that I had no male chauvinists as bosses. Other places in the company were different, but I had a lot of support from people I worked with.'

She was a single parent which, she says, if anything, helped: 'They knew I was the only breadwinner, so I was less risk. Some men have still to be convinced that women work for a career, not for pin money.'

'As Chairperson of the Equal Opportunities Committee, I feel the initiatives and recommendations now being made by both management and the committee are a positive step in the development and career prospects of all staff, including my own personal career.'

Another secretary who made her way into senior management is Sally Ryle, the Head of Publicity and Public Relations: 'I have never found being a woman at Yorkshire a problem. I've been very lucky and been given the opportunities in my department.' There were teething problems at the time: 'They were very bad on company car policy – they thought women shouldn't have company cars. That's changed now. Also, I was promoted fairly quickly and they put me on trial; because I had started off as a secretary they were worried about whether I could do the job or not. Had a man been given the job there would have been no question of putting him on trial.'

There was only a little hiccup when she took up her management position. She received a circular letter which said: 'Dear Sir, Would you like to put your wife and children on to private health insurance?' She says: 'It did annoy me. I took it up and the man concerned did apologise. I know that sort of thing doesn't happen now.'

Ms Ryle was also the first member of management to have a baby: 'They have been very good. The first time I was worried they would think: "That's what happens when we promote women." It was not like that at all. There was not even any question about my being able to keep the company car. My deputy just took over while I was away.

'The second time my immediate boss thought "Oh no! Not again." But there was no bad feeling.' Both times she took advantage of the thirteen weeks leave on full salary, which is standard in independent television companies. The toughest thing about going back was the pressure she imposed on herself: 'Women do overcompensate. I was determined that having children would not make any difference to my working life. I felt I had to prove myself because I was the first one in management.'

Diana Muir, who is in her late thirties, is a researcher in the Documentaries Department. Like all researchers now, she has been hired on a series of rolling contracts. After two and a half years, with one break of her own choosing, she has yet to see whether Yorkshire will put her on staff. In the brief time she has been in the department, she has noticed that increasing numbers of women are being promoted to producers, whereas when she first arrived there were very few: 'I suspect things are changing, partly because there have been changes of personalities here. Now it's a different generation with different attitudes.'

Whether those different attitudes will mean that the aspirations of the Equal Opportunities Committee can be met is yet to be seen. As Sue Seager from the Personnel Department and a member of the committee, says: 'The difficulty is that we do not have a recruitment problem, people are banging on the door to get in. Yet it still makes good business sense to get the best out of our women staff and keep them working for us.'

OIL COMPANIES

The British Petroleum Company plc is the parent company of one of the world's largest international petroleum and petrochemical groups. The company's key strengths are in oil and gas exploration, production, refining and marketing, and the manufacturing and marketing of chemicals. BP employs about 30,000 people in the UK: in its oil refineries and chemical plants, on the oil rigs and platforms, and at its headquarters, Britannic House in the City of London. Almost a fifth (19 per cent) of its workers are women.

British Petroleum (BP)

Equal Opps Policy	✓	Crèche	(3 planned)	✓
Equal Opps Recruitment	✓	Career Breaks		✓
Monitoring	✓	Jobshares	(support staff)	✓
Positive Action	✓	Flexible Hours		✓

Superficially, BP is an unlikely company to be a good employer of women: the image of the oil industry is consciously macho. None of the six managing directors is a woman, and only 2 per cent of senior management and 8 per cent of senior staff are women. However, it is a company which is making great efforts to change its ways.

Until the 1980s there were very few women graduate recruits. Now a quarter of them are female. It is from this pool that most of management is picked, so the opportunities should be there for women.

Vivienne Cox joined as a graduate nine years ago and is now, in her early thirties, the Manager of Derivative Products. She works on setting the long-term price of crude oil and its products for fixed-price energy contracts. She says: 'My prospects are good. A career path is open to me and there is nothing to stop me taking advantage of these openings. Although oil is traditionally a man's world, I don't think the company has an anti-female bias. I have never come across any corporate discrimination. In many ways quite the reverse.'

She has done well out of the company, having been sponsored to go for a year to INSEAD, at Fountainebleau in France, one of the top European business schools, to take her post-graduate business degree. Although there are many opportunities for training, Ms Cox thinks the company does not plan it very well: 'In some areas of the company training is random; whether the right people go on the right courses at the right time is rather left to chance.'

BP certainly takes equal opportunities seriously. Vicky Wisher has been developing the policy – and putting it into practice – since 1984. She is particularly heartened by the increase in the numbers of ethnic minority graduates being recruited: 'This is very encouraging, but we need to make sure it is maintained. And it's disappointing that we are not getting a good result from Afro-Caribbeans even though the response from Asians has been excellent. It is partly a result of the schools system and Afro-Caribbeans being expected to fail.'

Recruitment has been overhauled so that, in theory anyway, women are as likely as men to be recruited for good jobs. There is a booklet for all interviewers, as well as selection technique training. Advertising is also monitored.

To provide women with a means for self-help in BP there is WIBP – Women in BP – which was formed in 1982 by a group of women and is funded by BP. It aims to have twice monthly meetings in London and has set up regional sub-groups in Glasgow and Hemel Hempstead, Hertfordshire. Preliminary groups are being established in Sullom Voe in the Shetland Islands, Wytch Farm in Dorset, Aberdeen, Sunbury on Thames in Middlesex and Houston, Texas. All these groups run their own meetings. In London they range from informal lunches to evening workshops, with subjects ranging from childcare options to women, Europe and the 1990s. The group also invites speakers to talk on such subjects as self-defence, assertiveness and stress management.

BP encourages women to stay on after having a baby with enhanced maternity pay and career breaks. On top of standard maternity pay, women who have been with the company for over two years will get an extra month's pay for every year of service up to six years. The extra is paid as a lump sum three months after returning to work.

Career breaks are available for looking after young children, including adopted children. They can be taken as a complete break for months or even years, or as other alternatives to full-time office work in the form of part-time or flexible working hours, working partly from home, project work at home or jobsharing.

Janet Hogben has had two children while at BP and says she was treated well both times. But her praise is slightly guarded: 'It was more a function of who I knew, rather than company policy. The first time I asked for a job that didn't have long hours. I got a good job when I returned, as I had a helpful boss. But it wasn't frontline.

'I had the second child fairly soon after and asked to be transferred to Hemel Hempstead from the City because it was nearer to my home; I also wanted to go part-time and was ready to resign if I didn't get it. I felt I had to go to the brink. I did get a good part-time job in personnel, but personnel is not high profile in BP.

'You don't get on the frontline unless you work full-time and put in long hours.'

Ms Hogben says there is a 'long hours culture' at BP: 'Until people at the top and those in middle management demonstrably have a balanced life, new people come in, quickly see which behaviour is rewarded and emulate it.'

She is a now the manager of Exchanges in the supply function of BP Oil UK. It is an area responsible for negotiating and operating agreements with third parties and is definitely frontline. She says she tries to set standards and reward people for other attributes than long hours: 'There is a macho thing here that people are judged by their input. My saying is: "judge me by my output".'

Ms Hogben works approximately 8 a.m. to 6 p.m. which is made possible by living close to Hemel Hempstead and having a large support network of nanny, au pair, husband and family. By moving offices she saved herself over an hour's commuting time. However, to pursue her career seriously she says she must return to Britannic House in the City and be prepared to take the whole family abroad, raising yet more difficulties because there are two careers to consider.

Vivienne Cox works long hours but she finds the hours manageable and insists on a proper social life as well: 'I don't work weekends at all. It's a personal philosophy. I go sailing.'

BP treats its graduate women well but fares less well with its non-graduates – the vast majority of its female workforce. Given the right training and encouragement, many women who come in as secretaries or administrators could progress, but they are not given any opportunity to do so.

Janet Hogben thinks there still needs to be a fundamental attitude shift in BP before opportunities are really equal: 'I have come to believe the only way the great wodge of middle management will change is through targets. You need to get a significant number of women in there to influence people and be role models.'

Both women stress the pleasure they get out of working for BP. Ms Hogben says: 'Very nice people are employed here. There's a good salary and good working conditions. You can anticipate changing jobs every two years; I enjoy new work and that's the big attraction.'

Ms Cox says: 'I know I could earn more if I left but I enjoy what I do. There are real responsibilities and the people I have working for me are highly motivated.'

BP has made a commitment to recruiting skilled graduate women and encouraging them to pursue their careers as well as to have children if they so wish. While it needs to expand its horizons to explore the potential of less qualified women, in the targeted areas it has certainly been successful.

Esso supplies about a fifth of the petroleum products used in the UK and produces some 15 per cent of the country's total oil and gas output. The headquarters are in London, but most of the departments are at the offices in Leatherhead, Surrey. Esso has a refinery at Fawley, near Southampton, and a research centre near Abingdon in Oxfordshire. Esso employs about 4,000 people, the majority of these are in 'traditional male' roles like refinery operators, craftsmen and tanker drivers. Nonetheless women are approaching 15 per cent of employees. During the 1980s the number of women in managerial and professional jobs has trebled and it continues to grow.

Esso

Equal Opps Policy	✓	Crèche	✗
Equal Opps Recruitment	✓	Career Breaks	✓
Monitoring	✓	Jobshares	✗
Positive Action	✗	Flexible Hours	✓

In 1987 Esso was a finalist in the Women in Management (WIM) Equal Opportunity Employer awards. WIM is a support group for women in management and those aspiring to it, it is dedicated to raising the quality of managerial practices. Esso has continued to follow up its initiatives, both in promoting able women and allowing them to combine family and career.

The process begins with a recruitment policy designed to stop Esso being such a male-dominated company. In 1988, a third of graduate recruits were women, increasing to nearly half in 1989. June Harper, Corporate Planning and Investment Manager, says there is no tokenism: 'I have been involved in graduate recruitment and have recruited some excellent women engineers. They were employed because they were the best candidates for the job. Many of the women come across better in interviews than their male counterparts, having greater confidence and demonstrating more maturity.'

She says the problem has always been getting women to apply for a job in the industry in the first place: 'When I left university thirteen years ago, most of my women colleagues would not apply for jobs in industry because they thought they would not be accepted. For years there used to be few applications from women. A combination of things have changed: the culture, in that women are more independent and want careers; and more women are studying engineering and are now keen to apply to industry, and the industry is making a significant effort to attract high-quality people of both sexes.'

Miss Harper has been very successful with Esso and says she has never experienced discrimination: 'My last job was managing Esso's largest oil terminal in Europe. Esso is not interested in whether you are a man or a woman. If you prove yourself it will reward you with more responsibility.'

She has also encouraged the women coming up behind her: 'At West London terminal, there are three women supervisors. All three were appointed because they were best for the job.'

Miss Harper believes that in any organisation there is unconscious discrimination, but says essentially that can be overcome by doing a good job and having the ambition to succeed. She believes she can go far: 'I do want a good career. I do want to be a Divisional Director. I don't see why I shouldn't be.'

Valerie Macorison, a Senior Tax Adviser, says Esso has had a problem promoting women into executive management. This is the glass ceiling women will have to break through before the company proves itself truly woman-friendly. Ms Macorison does not expect to be the pioneer who breaks through because she is part-time. Since Nicholas was born three years ago, she has worked a three-day week. She organised it with Personnel and her own department before her return from maternity leave and it has never caused any problems. She considers that the arrangement will need to change when Nicholas goes to school, possibly becoming five short days. It works so well that, at present, she cannot envisage herself going back to full-time work. She is the most senior part-time woman in the company.

'I knew I could not come back full-time and my only other option was a career break, which is for up to five years. It is not valid for somebody with my specialisation because my knowledge would get out of date. Even the time I took out on maternity leave means there is one bit of legislation I do not feel quite familiar with.'

June Harper makes the point that women going on career breaks or part-time cannot expect to keep up with their peers. It will be a few years before it is possible to tell whether this is true as career breaks have been operating in Esso, and most other companies, for such a short time. Ms Macorison's view is that falling behind matters less than the expectation that people should be at a certain place on the ladder at a certain age, and they are looked at suspiciously if they have not arrived there on schedule: 'On the other hand, the company is very happy to push through young people. There are younger people than me who are higher up than me – men, of course.'

Jane Cox, a Quality Manager working in Leatherhead, says that she too has not encountered any obvious discrimination: 'I worked five years in a refinery and never came across it. The only problem was the lack of safety equipment of my size – I'm 5' nothing – so they sent out for it.'

She came back full-time after the birth of her son, Lindsay, seven months ago and has not encountered any problems. She was allowed to take six months off, and this helped a lot. Esso's maternity policy is for the first four months of the break to be on full pay. Like Valerie Macorison, she is not expected to do much overtime and both of them tend to work nine-hour days.

Esso surveyed the childcare needs of women managers in 1990 and found that there was a wide variety of requirements among them. Ms Cox says she would either like a nursery at the Fawley refinery, where her husband works, or a financial package to help with the cost of childcare.

All three women find the work fascinating which, combined with the working conditions, means they intend to make it a lifetime career. Valerie Macorison says: 'I find it difficult to envisage where I would find such an interesting job with the flexibility they have given me.'

Esso appears determined to recruit women into management

and encourage them to progress. While female managers and graduate trainees are particularly targeted, maternity benefits and career breaks are available to all women. As in all companies, it is more difficult to be promoted from clerical and secretarial grades, but it does happen. The future in Esso appears to offer enormous opportunities for women.

*Shell UK Ltd is the largest operating company in the Royal
Dutch Shell Group outside North America. The headquarters
are in London with plants throughout the UK. Shell sells
about 20 per cent of this country's petrol and other oil
products, produces 15 per cent of North Sea Oil and Gas and
is a major producer of chemicals as well. Shell UK Ltd
employs about 12,500 people, 2,200 of whom are female.*

Shell

Equal Opps Policy	✓	Crèche	✗
Equal Opps Recruitment	✓	Career Breaks	✓
Monitoring	✓	Jobshares	✓
Positive Action	✓	Flexible Hours	✓

Shell follows the pattern of the oil industry: it is a male dominated,
conservative company with extremely good policies for women
and a genuine determination to get the best out of the female
staff.

Lesley Secker is a Business Manager for Shell Chemicals UK
in Chester. She has worked for Shell for three years and has been
in the chemicals business for ten years: 'The graduate intake in
chemicals marketing has risen to around 50:50, as more women are
becoming interested in joining the industry.'

She also believes women are the better applicants: 'I am
definitely not a feminist, but I do think the women graduates are
more mature, more capable of delivering the job, quicker – they
are just a higher standard of applicant.'

Ms Secker makes presentations to students which she says is a
good way of encouraging women applicants: 'It's not necessarily
the policies which have the most impact on the females – though
perhaps they read those later – but students like to see women
who have got on. They like to see the proof that Shell does deliver.'

In the three years Ms Secker has been with Shell, she has been promoted twice. She is single and does not plan to have children, but the company appreciates that many women managers do want to mix family and career. It offers a range of flexible work options, including part-time work and working from home, and a career break which is particularly good because employees accepted onto the scheme are guaranteed redundancy at the end of the break if the company does not offer them comparable jobs. Uptake is not high at the moment, but it is expected to grow.

Mary Parsons is a Planning Analyst in the London headquarters who has been with the company for nine years. She returned to work four months after the birth of baby Nicole to an arrangement of two days in London and three days at home: 'I am involved in long-term planning for Distribution, one of the main activities being to assess the economics of our oil depots using computer models. I have a computer at home connected to the main frame at Shell. I had three main options for returning to work under Shell's maternity policy – one was to take off only eighteen weeks in total, one was to return within twenty-nine weeks of Nicole's birth and the third was to apply for a career break of up to two years. I chose the first as it allowed me to continue in the same job, which gave me the opportunity to work from home, and also meant that I received full pay and holiday entitlement during my absence.

'Returning to work so quickly has been made easier because of the flexible working arrangements. The days I am working at home I take Nicole to a childminder from 8 a.m. to 2.30 p.m. I then spend the afternoon with her and work another two or three hours in the evening when she's in bed. As I have a one-and-a-half-hour journey each way to London, I would not see her at all if I were there full-time. However, I do like going in a couple of days a week. Generally, I'm very pleased with the way it works.

'Although there was no set policy for flexible working in my department, the idea was received reasonably well and my line managers have been very supportive. Shell does quite nicely out of it too as I definitely feel I get more done than before. Once I sit down to start the day's work there are fewer interruptions than there would be in the office. There's also a tendency with working at home to work longer, as it's sometimes difficult to switch off.'

Staff have set up a Working Parent Group, which is open to men and women to discuss issues like these: the company supports the group. Shell has recently increased the amount of maternity leave on full pay to six months, with all benefits continued for women with over two years service.

Ms Parson joined the company as a Chemical Engineer, working in the Essex refinery. At that time she says there was a question mark over how women would progress as engineers and at one stage she was the only woman engineer at the refinery. She says there has been quite a change since then and that there are now a number of women in senior positions in engineering and as Plant Managers in the company.

Women graduates are a favoured species, but less-qualified women find it quite tough. Bernadette Smith is an Assistant in Employment Policy with a 1-year-old boy, Robert. She returned to full-time work after eighteen weeks paid maternity leave. She did not consider going part-time, partly for financial reasons.

In the ten years she has worked at Shell Ms Smith has felt that being a non-graduate many doors were just not open to her. Unfortunately, she was pregnant when the first course came up to help non-graduates to improve their career development opportunities. In addition to such programmes, there is also a two-day workshop for women, Stepping Stones, to help personal development.

Overall Ms Smith applauds these efforts: 'The company is trying but I'm not sure it's succeeding in advertising what options can be made available to women. I'm in personnel so I know what's around, other women may not. For instance, I knew I could ask to work part-time. We need to educate line managers.'

She thinks it will be the young women high-flyers of today who will change Shell, 'although I think it will take time to get the first woman on the board'.

Ms Secker agrees that changes in Shell will be 'evolutionary not revolutionary', as women graduate recruits climb the ladder: 'It's a fairly slow process, as the women work through.' At 31, she is the most senior woman in Shell Chemicals UK.

As Ms Secker says: 'An awful lot of thought goes into the development of policies. The oil business is a group of pretty high-performing companies, all competing with each other for the top people, many of those are women.' Shell, like the other good oil companies, demonstrates what can be achieved in a male-dominated, conservative industry, with good employment policies and determination. The company shows that trying to adapt to individual needs reaps enormous dividends in keeping good employees.

PUBLIC AND PRIVATE SERVICES

The British Council promotes Britain abroad. It promotes British ideas, skills and experience - in education, the English language, the arts, sciences and technology - in both developing and industrialised countries. It has 4,400 staff in the UK and over eighty countries around the world; over half of them are women. The headquarters are in London, with a new British Council North to be opened in Manchester in 1992. There is a choice between the Home Careers Service and the Overseas Careers Service.

The British Council

Equal Opps Policy	✓	Crèche (Planned)	✓
Equal Opps Recruitment	✓	Career Breaks	✓
Monitoring	✓	Jobshares	✓
Positive Action	✓	Flexible Hours	✓

The British Council, which promotes the best of British, also appears to practice some of the best initiatives in equal opportunities and these are slowly permeating throughout its ranks.

At the top, the Council is male dominated: only three of the twenty-three board members and a mere 5 per cent of senior management are women. Middle management, however, consisting of half women, half men, does begin to reflect the make-up of the organisation; 76 per cent of junior management are female, showing that the various equal opportunity policies are making their mark.

The Council has examined its recruitment policies carefully, and gives specific training to anyone involved in recruitment. The application form no longer asks for first names, school attended, dependents or marital status. The shortlisting is as objective as possible and women are well represented among the recruiters.

Rebecca Walton is Deputy Head of Recruitment for the Overseas Careers Service where staff have postings for three years to any one of eighty countries, ranging from Greece to Indonesia; they are expected to spend two-thirds of their career overseas. She says that most of the women with partners find they are willing to follow the Council's posting – because the partners tend to be teachers or aid workers. Only married couples get the generous allowances available for spouses, co-habitees are ineligible. There is long recruitment process for the overseas service so that applicants can properly consider what they are getting into. The Council thinks it is discriminatory to bring up specifically the problem women might have of sustaining a relationship when they are travelling round the world, but Rebecca Walton adds: 'We allow them to talk to us about it if they want, or they can talk to another Personnel Officer not involved in their recruiting for more confidentiality.'

Ms Walton asked for and was given a home posting after giving birth at the end of her previous posting in Norway, but she is happy to go abroad again. Her husband does pursue a career in Britain, but she says he can be more flexible than most people because he is an academic with sabbaticals and long summer vacations.

Over the last two years half of the people recruited to the Overseas Careers Service have been women, compared to about 8 per cent in the early 1980s. The Council has been encouraging women to join because the Overseas Careers Service is the best route to top management positions.

Ms Walton says that when she goes to working mothers groups, 'they are speechless at how well I am treated. There is a serious commitment to making life for a working mother as easy as possible. Something which may appear minor, like being able to take time off for a sick child, is tremendously important.'

There are plans for a crèche at the future Manchester

headquarters; a childcare policy is being established for all UK based staff. For overseas postings childcare and domestic help is organised, and school fees are paid if parents choose to send their children back to this country.

The Council give eight weeks more maternity leave than the statutory minimum of twenty-nine weeks and provide both jobsharing and career break schemes. Most women return after having children. Flexi-time is already operating, and the Council is about to introduce reduced hours and term-time working only for parents with children at school, possibly restricted to lower grades or jobs. Homeworking is being considered. Some jobs which used to be full-time have become part-time when a department's needs have changed, and more movement from full-time to part-time is expected.

About fifty women have been on career breaks, which are up to seven years for looking after children or relatives; four have returned, five have resigned. Unpaid leave may also be granted if a member of staff has to accompany their spouse whose work takes them overseas, or if a member of staff wants to study on a full-time course.

There are thirty teams of jobsharers, including two men, and these are concentrated in junior and lower middle-management positions. However, the Council is trying to encourage more jobsharing and more part-time posts higher up the ladder. Lydia Parbury is one of the more senior jobsharers, managing a section with nine people. She works the first half of every week. She decided to jobshare when her disabled son went to a special school and she wanted to play a bigger part in his education. Although there was reluctance when she first tried to set up the post as a jobshare, there have been no problems since. She feels this will not hinder her promotion prospects.

Debbie Simmons is another jobshare who has no children but wanted to do voluntary work and pursue other interests rather than work for the Council full-time. She did not have to give any specific reasons to be allowed to jobshare. She works in the Home Career Service, helping to match the education needs of developing countries with expertise in the UK. She went full-time for two months to go to Indonesia. She has also taken a year's unpaid leave to go and teach English in Zimbabwe: 'The Council agreed because they thought I would benefit if I had more experience in developing countries. Most people return with renewed vigour and energy. Going away for a while does make one realise it's an interesting job.'

Promotion at the British Council is slow, particularly in the Home Career Service, where the pay, which is at Civil Service levels, is kept down. Positive initiatives aim at getting more women into senior management positions, and the complaint is more of log jams than any bias against women.

Rebecca Walton says it is the diversity of people that makes working for the Council so special: 'It would be hard to find an environment where people are more friendly and interesting.'

The British Council certainly does not offer run-of-the-mill jobs, and for those in the Overseas Careers Service it entails as Rebecca Walton put it 'giving some career structure to people with wanderlust'. Most important is a genuine attempt to allow able women to rise with their ability and not to have to make a choice between career and motherhood.

British Rail is a national passenger, freight and parcels railway system which operates in England, Scotland and Wales. It employs 130,000 people all over the country – about 10,000, or 8 per cent, of this total are women.

British Rail

Equal Opps Policy	✓	Crèche	✗
Equal Opps Recruitment	✓	Career Breaks	✓
Monitoring	✓	Jobsharing	✓
Positive Action	✓	Flexible Hours	✓

During the 1980s British Rail joined with the Equal Opportunities Commission to discover what changes were necessary to encourage more women to join the company. The research showed a lack of opportunity for women at all levels and questioned whether British Rail's employment practices were consistent with the company's goals of 'quality and people first'.

Lesley Holland, the first British Rail Equal Opportunities Manager, who has since left, said there was a clear commitment to equal opportunities at board and director level: 'The challenge was to get that message across the spectrum of British Rail employees, up to a level where it would permeate the everyday actions of the business. Ninety-three per cent of British Rail employees were male. Employment practices were traditional and designed by men with men in mind. For change to take place in British Rail, men had to make them happen. To make progress in equal opportunities, it was essential to foster the will to change within the organisation.'

British Rail developed an action plan to promote fair and effective practice, which set out a timetable for changes. They accepted that there was little point in increasing the number of women employees if nothing was done to change the workplace environment in order to make it a comfortable place for women and a better place for everyone.

Enormous strides have been made in the last five years. Targets have been set for the recruitment of both graduate and non-graduate women, and for promotion. Equal opportunities are included in basic supervisory and disciplinary training. There are courses for women seeking to get into management, and there are self-development courses for women. Career breaks are now offered to all staff.

Linda Phipps, in her mid-thirties, is now Marketing Manager of Network South-East. She joined in 1976 and says conditions for women have improved tremendously: 'It was dreadful when I first went there. Now women can have a go at anything, but there is still a male bias. When a woman does something there is a sense of amazement. There are very, very few women in front-line jobs. Specialised jobs are OK for women – personnel, public relations, even, I suppose, marketing – but there is an attitude that a woman couldn't actually run a railway. I'm very pleased that some of my friends are working in Operations and Engineering, changing that perception by being good "at the job".'

Ms Phipps has also tested British Rail's attitude to women with families and been extremely well treated. When she became pregnant with her second daughter, she discussed various childcare options with her director and opted for a nursery which they both felt was more reliable than a nanny, although it restricted her hours. She had not bargained for the attitude of outer London Conservative local authorities, many of which are loath even to licence private nurseries because they believe that mothers of young children should stay at home. She found a nursery that was an hour's drive from home, but also an hour from work – entailing four hours travelling a day. Her working day was 9.30 a.m. to 4.30 p.m. which she found too short, and it was difficult to catch up in the evenings. Now she has found a nursery closer to her home which is open longer hours, and her boss knows that when the chips are down she will go home and work all night to ensure the work is done.

'Before the baby I used to do fifty-five to sixty hours a week. This has made me realise I didn't spend enough time with my elder daughter. I was working an unreasonable time. Now I have learnt to delegate. The nursery is a discipline: I can't work until

9 p.m., so I must structure my time more firmly.

'I think I'm relatively special; special in that I've decided to drive a bargain. I think I'm the first executive grade woman to produce a child in office. There are few women in British Rail, few senior women and even fewer senior women with children. It's a very male organisation. Most women wouldn't dare ask for special treatment: but I am a worker and a mother. I do feel a certain sense of breaking the mould. If I can make it work then others can do it.'

Linda Phipps has worked her way up British Rail, although as a graduate entrant she was always on the fast track. The Assistant Director of the Quality Programme, Susan Hoyland, was specifically head-hunted to be a Public Relations Manager for BR: 'I was 42, an advanced age, my children were almost grown up and I was running the pressure group Transport 2000. My pay there was very low, so it was easy for BR to double my salary, although that isn't why I came here.'

Still feeling something of an outsider after three years, she says: 'It's a very large, very old industry. There's an enormous tradition of family loyalty, father to son. There's strength to that loyalty but it was difficult when it came to saying we should employ more women. People would say: "There's never been a woman doing that job, except during the war – and that didn't count." It's a huge task but I don't doubt the sincerity of the policy or the people pursuing that policy. I feel comfortable working here.

'At my level there are very few women and there is little prejudice. The number of women in senior management has virtually quadrupled because of gender targets: on the whole we have been recruited from outside. Women who work as drivers or guards may have had different experiences.'

British Rail's commitment to training, particularly the many women-only courses, should see more women coming through the organisation to take up managerial positions. BR is also encouraging more women to apply for all jobs by considering where to place advertisements to attract women applicants. Susan Hoyland thinks that the greatest problem is getting women to apply, as British Rail is perceived as a male organisation: 'If more women apply more will be likely to get appointed.' The key to making British Rail more woman-friendly is getting more women into the system: a task the management is taking very seriously.

*British Telecom is one of Europe's largest companies, with a
turnover in 1989/90 in excess of £12 billion. It serves 25
million customers in the UK and handles over 80 million
phone calls a day. It also has a range of products and
services for transmitting voice, data, text and pictures both in
the UK and beyond. The range of jobs include business
management, information technology, engineering and
research and technology. British Telecom has 232,000
employees who are mostly based in regional centres all over
the country. Of these 68,000 are women.*

British Telecom

Equal Opps Policy	✓	Crèche	✗
Equal Opps Recruitment	✓	Career Breaks	✓
Monitoring	✓	Jobshares	✓
Positive Action	✗	Flexible Hours	✓

British Telecom needs skilled people, and like all other companies
once people have been recruited BT wants them to stay on.
Traditionally it has been a male-oriented company, but in the last
decade it has realised the importance of women.

One of British Telecom's innovative schemes is to offer
scholarships to its employees to do research which will ultimately
benefit the company. Victoria Hillier won an award to investigate
women in management, focusing on operational engineering
management. She travelled to the USA and Sweden to compare
experiences abroad with those in the UK. Now the company is
beginning to make practical use of her findings: the first step is
to destroy the myth that one has to be a man to be an engineering
manager; the second is to question whether one even needs to be
an engineer.

Ms Hillier says: 'If you look at the job, it's essentially about
managing human resources; one can go on a training course to

appreciate the technical content. We need to open the door to non-graduates and women working their way up the company from somewhere like sales. We want to make better use of the female resources we've already got. We want women to be at all levels of management. We have to do more than just call ourselves an equal opportunities employer. We have to take positive steps to make that happen.'

Only a quarter of BT's employees are women, yet in 1989 over half of the new recruits were female. So, the gender profile of the company is changing: a lot of the effort is being put into training. There are women-only courses, and a lot of in-house technical courses. Ms Hillier says: 'Training opportunities for personal and career development have not been targeted towards women, and attention to family considerations has been lacking. It is my belief that BT will respond sympathetically when problems are flagged up, but has not up to now designed policies with these issues in mind. Much depends on the local Personnel Manager and his or her attitude.

'In terms of management development opportunities for women, a joint venture is being run with Cranfield Institute of Technology. However, this is only the tip of the iceberg and the women who get on in the company do so through their own initiative or through having a "sponsor" – some senior person, normally male, who takes them under their wing.'

A women-only bridging course to prepare for a science degree started in 1987. There is also a development management programme to help people to become managers. This is more than a course because trainees are also given a mentor in the company for personal encouragement. The company has extended the upper age limit of the apprentice scheme by twenty-two years, from 19 to 41.

Sandra Wilkins, who works in Employee Communications in Reading, came in as a secretary four years ago: 'I was encouraged to stop being a secretary and start going for promotion. I went into Personnel, which I find much more rewarding. If they hadn't encouraged me out of secretarial I would still be there. Now I'm a junior manager.'

Ms Wilkins had the last of her three children while at BT: 'They

asked about children on the application form, but it was made clear
at the interview that it was not a problem. When I had another
baby they were very generous with maternity benefits and leave
time.'

The maternity package is generous. Women are given thirteen
weeks off on full pay – although five weeks pay is held back until
the mother has returned to work for thirteen weeks. Up to
eighteen months unpaid special leave may be requested after
maternity leave, and this is given at the discretion of individual
units. This special leave is a form of career break, and is mainly
open to management grades. The National Communications
Union, which organises many BT staff, negotiated a jobsharing
scheme in 1989 for its 200,000 members that is the largest in the
private sector. Previously there were only informal jobshares.
Jobshares have been mostly in sub-management positions and are
more likely to be given in districts like London and Thames Valley,
where there are shortages of skilled workers.

The NCU also negotiated flexi-time for its members, in line with
the long-established system for clerical workers. Some telephone
operators are now part-time. There is also an initiative to start
teleworking, which is operating a computer from home. However,
not much time appears to have been given to thinking about
reduced working hours, even for junior management.

Nevertheless, BT has a good reputation on hours. Sandra
Wilkins says she does not have to work long hours. Vanessa
Marshall, who is a Change Management Consultant also based in
Reading, says she works standard hours: 'Less than I used to
when I first came here two years ago, and if I work more I take
time off in lieu. I think hours are more important to me now than
when I first started: it's about getting my life in perspective.

'Working long hours rather than being effective is still rewarded.
However, one woman Level 3 Manager has two children and leaves
every day at 5.30 p.m. I think you're more effective if you can
manage your time within the proper working day. I respect that.'

Ms Marshall says the opportunities are good for women in BT:
'I was a graduate entrant and was promoted within ten months.
I think I could go higher if I wanted to: if you're good, you've got
an equal chance. Sex is not a factor.

'There are only a few, well-respected women above me. There are fewer as you get higher. It's the problem with being a technical organisation and tending to promote from within. They recruit boy apprentices. I think attitudes are changing slowly, but I don't know if actions are changing.'

British Telecom has come a long way in the last decade and is constantly looking at ways to use women more effectively and allow them to mix career and family. However, this is not evenly spread nationwide; women in the south-east of England get a better deal than women in the rest of the country.

*The Civil Service is concerned with the conduct of the whole
range of government activities as they affect the community,
ranging from policy formulation to carrying out the day-to-
day duties that public administration demands. The main
offices of most departments are based in London, but there are
offices around the country, where 80 per cent of the staff are
based. It has 500,000 employees, 45 per cent of whom are
women.*

The Civil Service

Equal Opps Policy	✓	Crèche	✓
Equal Opps Recruitment	✓	Career Breaks	✓
Monitoring	✓	Jobshares	✓
Positive Action	✓	Flexible Hours	✓

The Civil Service is probably the best employer of women in the
country. Years before equal opportunities were fashionable, the
Civil Service took a long hard look at what was happening to its
women employees and their findings were not encouraging.
Women rose through the ranks much more slowly than their male
counterparts and many left work after having children. Equal
opportunities posts were created in the Cabinet Office and
departments to devise policies to combat the barriers women
faced, and monitoring was introduced.

The recruitment of Civil Service 'high-flyers' and executive
officers was overhauled at the end of the 1980s, which led to a
significant increase in the success rate of women applicants. By
1989, women accounted for 43 per cent of successful candidates for
'fast track' administration and executive positions, compared with
29 per cent in 1985. However, women recruited into the fast stream
have a slower career progression than men. Half the male fast-
stream recruits in 1972 had reached Grade 5 level by 1987, while
only 14 per cent of the women had done so. Slowly the proportion

of women in the top grades is increasing and the Civil Service Commission is keeping it under review. The Civil Service believes this is a result of the flexible attitude to working mothers, which means women no longer have to choose between motherhood and furthering a career.

Diane Phillips, Under Secretary for the Department of the Environment, is one of the most senior women in the Civil Service. She is also part-time, working a four-day week: 'In 1981 I went part-time when I returned after the birth of my second child. I decided I had proved the point that I could work full-time with a child. There was one six-month period when I went full-time in 1985: I had devised the Bill for the abolition of the Greater London Council and Metropolitan County Councils and when it went into Parliament I stuck around to get it through. Afterwards I took three months off.

'I think it's very important that people are allowed to work part-time. It is in the interests of both women and the department. When I work a five-day week, as I do occasionally, I come back on Monday much more stressed. With a four-day week, I am better able to concentrate. Part-time enables women to combine a job and raising a family more effectively than one otherwise could.'

Ms Phillips has been promoted twice since going part-time. She has successfully scuppered a lot of the prejudices against part-timers for the women coming up behind her: 'When I first asked for part-time I was the first Grade 5 to do it. A number of people have said I'm a good role model. Women thinking of having babies can see what they can aim for. They haven't got to trail blaze, they can follow a path.'

Susan Haird, Head of Personnel Management and the Equal Opportunities Division in the Cabinet Office, is another senior part-timer, doing two full days and three short days: 'It's wonderful, absolutely no problem, and I don't anticipate any in the future. Many of my colleagues have been working part-time for years. Ten per cent of the people at my level, Grade 5, are part-timers.

'The arrangements do not even seem to be very complex. In some departments there are not enough part-timers to go round, because many jobs can be done by part-timers' work. This is certainly the case in the Department of Trade and Industry where I come from. Part-time is so widespread partly because of an enlightened management and partly because women are demanding it. There are a lot of middle-management, articulate, well-educated, prized women who would not stay if they were not being offered part-time. The size of the Civil Service helps as jobs are constantly changing in response to ministerial needs.'

At the Inland Revenue the promotion of part-timers is being monitored. Carolyn Hubbard, the Chief Equal Opportunities Officer, says in practice there are no barriers: 'In the Revenue, promotion is through technical training. At one time we only trained full-time people, which meant women could only progress if they came back full-time. Now the full technical training is available part-time. One woman has done an Accounts Investigation course part-time and been promoted to Inspector of Taxes.'

For some women, the problem is wanting to come back full-time but not having flexibility with working hours because of family commitments. Hilary Watkins was working for the Health and Safety Executive in a job which involved considerable travel, including trips to Luxembourg to discuss European proposals affecting the mining and quarrying industries. When her husband was relocated to Bristol, leaving her as the sole parent of three children during the week, she needed a job with more regular hours and less travel. She was seconded to the Cabinet Office and is now responsible for developing and encouraging departments to implement equal opportunities policies for women and people with disabilities.

Ms Watkins is also a woman returner who was recruited late, at the age of 41. She trained as a solicitor and gave up work to have a family, then joined the Citizen's Advice Bureau, first as a volunteer and later going full-time. She applied for the Civil Service because she thought it would be challenging, with the bonus of having reasonable employment conditions. She was put to work on health and safety legislation for mines and quarries: 'I couldn't think of anything further from my experience.' But she loved it.

She stresses how the Civil Service differs from its image: 'The picture that people have of the Civil Service is a lot of grey folk pushing paper. While there is a lot of paper it is a much more people-oriented job than it is usually given credit for. It is very difficult to get stale because there is always the possibility of something new. The basic structure is designed to be supportive to staff. I think the general basis on which the Civil Service works is not treating its people as automata. There are few places where I've worked where people laugh so much.

'It seems to me that although the Civil Service is not in the lead in any one particular area as an employer, overall we are in the lead. We try and cover all the options.'

All schemes aimed at helping mothers to combine work with children, such as part-time working and career breaks, are open to women throughout the Civil Service whatever their level. The Civil Service policy is that everybody is treated on merit and should be able to rise regardless of the level they entered the organisation. In fact, women's promotion rates from the bottom are not equal to men. There is no obvious reason for this apart from the fact that many more women leave than men. Hilary Watkins believes that as career breaks and part-time working allow increasing numbers of women to continue their careers the numbers of women rising from the ranks will grow: 'I'm sure we shall see a real improvement.'

Equal opportunities initiatives, such as optional part-time working for senior positions, which are taken for granted in the Civil Service, are still considered beyond the pale in many organisations that consider themselves to be progressive. The Civil Service should not be dismissed as full of stuffy government bureaucrats but seen as a standard bearer for encouraging women to reach their full potential.

The National and Local Government Officers Association, or
NALGO as the union is more commonly known, represents
people working in local government, gas, electricity, the water
authorities, education and the Health Service. It is the UK's
third largest union with 750,000 members, half of whom are
women. Its headquarters are in Euston, north London and it
has district offices in England, Scotland and Wales. Over half
of the 1,000 staff are women.

National and Local Government Officers Association (NALGO)

Equal Opps Policy	✓	Crèche	✓
Equal Opps Recruitment	✓	Career Breaks	✓
Monitoring	✗	Jobshares	✓
Positive Action	✗	Flexible Hours	✓

Trade unions may be in the forefront of fighting for equal rights,
with many officers and lay officials putting in sterling work.
Indeed, some of the results may have ensured certain companies
a place in this book, but it is significant that NALGO is the only
union included here. Trade unions do not provide particularly well
for the women who work for them. Even those unions representing mainly women have male General Secretaries. Only two trade
unions in this country have women General Secretaries: the First
Division (for top civil servants) and the Association of University
Teachers.

NALGO has led the way in getting many local authorities to
adopt progressive equal opportunities policies and has sought to
put its own house in order. It is certainly a union run by men: the
General Secretary, Deputy General Secretary and two Assistant
General Secretaries are all male, along with most of the National
Officers. The Personnel Office says there is a low proportion of
women in supervisory and managerial grades, but it cannot give

accurate figures until the Records Department is computerised.

Ada Maddocks, the National Officer for Health and a member of the TUC General Council, is about to retire from the union after thirty years. She started as a secretary to a National Officer in the Electricity Section and worked her way up to become the first woman National Officer in NALGO: 'I think there has been a big improvement in the appointment of women on the staff. There used not to be women District Officers. People in head office were worried about them having to travel and be alone; now there are quite a few.'

Like Ada Maddocks, Elaine Harrison, National Officer for Higher Education, remembers the debate over women District Officers when she started. While that battle has been won, she worries about women's prospects overall: 'There are a lot of women in the lower officers grades, doing case work and negotiations, but the senior tasks are mostly done by men. In the short term, I do not see it altering; but as we get better recruitment and selection procedures more and better women will be coming in at the bottom. At present, there is not even a proper equal opportunities strategy of recruitment or monitoring. We are discussing it with the staff unions.'

Alison Mitchell, Deputy National Officer for Local Government, summed up the situation: 'There tends to be an element of Buggins' turn and women have to wait longer to be Buggins.'

Ms Mitchell also noted that there is a low proportion of women in senior jobs and an even lower proportion with children; neither Ada Maddocks nor Elaine Harrison have them.

NALGO does have excellent conditions for returning mothers, offering places in a nearby crèche and an allowance which is graded in terms of salary. Childcare costs for work outside normal hours and attendance on training courses are available for children under 14. Crèches are sometimes provided on weekend courses.

Ms Mitchell, a mother of two, said NALGO was good in terms of childcare help: 'But, like most organisations, there is a tendency to think once they are 5 they can go to school alone, come home alone, make the tea and look after themselves at weekends.'

She says NALGO must give more consideration to women returning from maternity leave: 'I came back after my second and was immediately expected to go away a lot, instead of being allowed to adjust. It was partly my fault because I wanted to prove I was able and somehow I coped.'

She finds that the greatest problem for women at NALGO is common to all trade unions: 'They are very difficult for women - lots of work goes on outside the office. There is still a macho style to the way people do the job. It took me a long time to realise I did not have to do it that way. I did not have to bullshit in meetings. A lot of women below me feel they do not want to go up any further because they do not want to be like these men. Among the men there is a competitiveness and unwillingness just to knock ideas about.'

Elaine Harrison believes the style is changing: 'But it has taken nearly two decades and even then there is not as great a change as I would like to see. But as far as the working environment goes, it is less macho than many other unions. They certainly employ more women.'

In spite of criticisms they both agree it is the best union to work for as a woman. Although the emphasis appears to be on making it as easy as possible to combine parenthood and a career rather than concentrating on the perennial problem of women under-achieving at work, which is as endemic at NALGO as everywhere else.

National Health Service

The National Health Service has ¾ million women on its staff in the UK; this makes it the biggest employer of women in Europe. While individual health authorities are doing some sterling work, overall the NHS has yet to prove its real commitment to equal opportunities for women.

Researchers point to the bad deal women have been getting for years in all parts of the service: men in every sector are likely to earn more and have a greater chance of promotion. The National Steering Group of Equal Opportunities for Women in the NHS says this situation alone justifies the development of an equal opportunities policy. Added to that, the group goes on to say, the NHS will have to adapt its policies to cope with the changing labour market if it hopes to attract more 'mature women and members of Black and ethnic minority communities'.

Isobel Allan, in her book *Any Room at the Top: A Study of Doctors and their Careers*, vividly describes how women doctors, from the students in medical school through to consultants, face sexist attitudes, the 'old boy network' of patronage, discriminatory questions at interviews and many other examples of less favourable treatment. Although a quarter of the doctors who graduated in the 1960s were women, now, almost thirty years on, only 13 per cent of hospital consultants are female and only 20 per cent of the principals in general practice. Some women left the profession because their career paths were consistently blocked or because it was impossible to combine the work with children, while most of those remaining opted for lower-status areas, like public health, as opposed to surgery.

Sadly, rigid, male-dominated hierarchies among doctors are almost taken for granted and this runs throughout the NHS. A lot of the responsibility for this state of affairs can be traced to the Salmon Report on the NHS which was published in 1966. The Salmon Report's conclusions are crucial to the rise of men in nursing. The Report criticised female authority and management skills; women, it concluded are unable to make administrative decisions. The qualities it set out as essential for management jobs – dynamism, rationality and tough-mindedness – were said to be uniquely male attributes. This led to men being encouraged to join the NHS, an area in which women had previously quietly thrived.

Celia Davies and Jane Rosser looked at the result of this change in *Processes of Discrimination: A Report on a Study of Women Working in the NHS*: it was, they found, bad news for women. For men, it took on average eight and a half years to get from initial qualification to the position of Nursing Officer; it took women almost eighteen years, and this time span did not include time out to bring up a family. The authors concluded 'men appeared to break all the rules - they entered late, they went to the "wrong" nursing schools, did not shine particularly in terms of qualifications, and yet they had progressed faster than women'.

For the clerical and administration grades, it was the same sorry story. Davies and Rosser found: 'A bottom heavy structure with men dominating the senior posts and women monopolising the large base of junior, administrative, clerical and secretarial grades ... Women were hardly to be found in more senior positions in those functions regarded as offering career potential.'

The report led the Minister of State for Health to set up a working group on Equal Opportunities in the NHS in 1986. The group's first report in 1987 contained another catalogue of depressing statistics, but it has also induced health authorities, at both regional and district level, to take equal opportunities seriously. There are now few Health Service Managers who will not pay lip service at least to women being taken seriously. No statistics have been released to demonstrate whether women are making their ways to the top, but there has been a move to look at working conditions and childcare facilities within the NHS.

As late as 1990 the Health Service unions have noted that the grading structure for NHS ancillary workers was 'fundamentally discriminatory and does not comply with the Equal Pay Act'. The four unions in the Health Service - National Union of Public Employes (NUPE), Confederation of Health Service Employees (COHSE), General, Municiple Boilermakers and Allied Trades Union (GMB) and the Transport and General Workers Union (TGWU) - argued that the job evaluation scheme carried out in the 1960s undervalued two major features of manual jobs carried out mainly by women: manual dexterity and stamina.

In early 1989, a survey entitled *Jobsharing in the NHS* by N. Meager, J. Buchan and C. Rees carried out by the Institute of Manpower Studies, showed that over half the health authorities and boards in the UK were employing some jobsharers, and the number was continuing to grow. The reasons for the creation of jobshares tended to be the need to recruit new employees and to keep them, or in response to an employee or union request, rather than as part of an equal opportunities policy. However, jobshares represent a step in the right direction.

Crèches and more flexible hours are being introduced, particularly in the South-east of England, where recruitment is increasingly more difficult as so many well-paid jobs are based there. But the NHS still has a long way to go if it is to do more than allow women to demonstrate overwhelming dedication in the face of little pay and even less respect.

There is a new breed of health authorities where equal
opportunities are beginning to be taken seriously. Croydon
District Health Authority is typical of these. The authority
runs the health services in the Croydon area. It has 5,900
employees, the vast majority of whom are women.

Croydon District Health Authority (CHA)

Equal Opps Policy	✓	Crèche	✗
Equal Opps Recruitment	✓	Career Breaks	✓
Monitoring	✓	Jobshares	✓
Positive Action	✗	Flexible Hours	✓

Croydon District Health Authority (CHA) has equal opportunity
policies which have arisen out of both necessity and
enlightenment. Because Croydon is situated on the south-west
fringes of London, skills are in short supply and they do not come
cheap: almost all staff know they can increase their salaries by
finding other employers.

It is necessary to recruit good staff and to keep them. This has
led CHA to adopt various flexible hours schemes, particularly for
nurses and secretaries. Individual contracts tailored to specific
needs are often drawn up. Jobsharing is more common among
secretarial staff than nurses but it is available to both types of
employee.

Career breaks are open to all staff, but it is necessary to have
worked for the Authority for two years to earn a career break for
domestic reasons. You need to have worked for the NHS for five
years, of which three have to have been with CHA, to qualify for
a study break. There are two schemes: a non-guarantee scheme
which gives an undertaking to re-employ if possible and to match
previous terms of employment as closely as possible for anybody
who is eligible; and a guarantee scheme which ensures that on
return, the person will be given the same or equivalent post, grade

and salary as before. This is only available at the manager's discretion for staff who are difficult to recruit.

There is a special mature entrance course for nurses that is specifically geared to mothers, with terms and half-terms matching school holidays and seven weeks unpaid leave in the summer. Monthly pay is the same over the whole year to ease financial difficulties during the break.

The Health Authority has started monitoring its employees on the grounds of gender and race, and has drawn up an action plan on ways of improving the status of both. Training and development of staff has been earmarked as a priority, and all managers and staff involved in recruitment will be trained in equal opportunities. Recruitment has also been overhauled.

The Authority is particularly good in that it has women in prominent positions. The District General Manager is female, the Director of Nursing Practice and Quality Assurance and the Director of Planning and Commissioning in the Authority's Mayday Hospital are women, as is the Director of the Community Health Service; there are also women in many other senior positions.

Judy Hargadon, Head of the Community Health Unit, sees her position both as a role model and a chance to allow working mothers like herself to juggle all parts of their lives successfully: 'I encourage flexible working hours and jobshares among Health Visitors – when I arrived in 1989 there was no flexibility. Some clerical staff work school terms only. Some people gather up time in lieu and take it regularly, while some take it at holiday time.

'I make it an absolute principle that I take the children to school once a week, which means that I am "late", to show we all have duties as parents. I make sure fathers have a chance to be flexible too, because I believe the reason so many working mothers have a hard time is that the fathers are given no flexibility in their work.'

Another feather in Croydon's cap is that they will promote secretaries, although the process is not easy. Like most other employers there are managers who doubt that secretaries have the potential to move.

Croydon has yet to complete its action plan to ensure real equality of opportunity but the authority is starting out from a good base.

RETAIL

Boots The Chemist started its pharmacy shops just over one hundred years ago and now has over a thousand stores in the UK. It employs 45,000 people, of whom 39,000, or 86 per cent, are women. The stores are still based on pharmacy, but now also include health care and beauty products. The head offices are in Nottingham.

Boots The Chemist

Equal Opps Policy	✓	Crèche	✗
Equal Opps Recruitment	✓	Career Breaks	✓
Monitoring	✓	Jobshares	✓
Positive Action	✗	Flexible Hours	✓

Boots encompasses some of the best and the worst aspects of the retail industry, but happily it is improving all the time. It has been a classic retail organisation, staffed mainly by women and run almost entirely by men. In the familiar high street stores, almost all the shop assistants are women – one employee said bitterly that no man would work for those wages – but most shop managers are men. This is now changing as increasing numbers of women are coming through the system. Boots also now has numerous schemes to encourage women to build a career in the company, and to return to work after having children.

Boots pioneered the Flexible Working Parents Contract, or term-time working as it is known elsewhere. These contracts allow women to choose their hours as well as take school holidays off. For Anne White, a Chemist-counter Assistant in Winchester, it changed her life – it allowed her to work: 'I used to do secretarial work and I couldn't go back to that. When my children were both at school I wanted to go back to work, but only school hours and term-time. I heard Boots were offering it.

'The great thing about it is that I'm made to feel just as much part of it as everybody else - same training, same perks, pro rata holiday. Not only do Boots do it, but they make you feel welcome. I never have to apologise for taking the holidays off.

'I might work more hours as time goes by. I've now got confidence in myself that I can work - that I am a marketable person. I was off work for about sixteen years.'

Mrs White has only praise for the effect Boots has had on her life, pointing out that it's 'absolutely wonderful' for women. She is particularly impressed by the training: 'They are very hot on training. They mind terribly that they train their staff properly. I have learnt such an amazing amount since I've been there; it makes you realise how important it is to get it right.'

It is not only shop assistants who benefit from flexible working. In Boots stores, Senior Assistants, Supervisors and Sales Managers have been able to jobshare since 1988. Previously, people on those grades were only permitted to work full-time because the management believed the jobs were too responsible to be shared. At the end of 1990, there were thirty jobshares and over 200 people on term-time contracts - with the idea gaining ground around the country.

There is a Women Returners Network, based at the Boots head office in Nottingham. It acts as both a support group for women returning to work after maternity leave, or a career break, and as a pressure group to make sure their needs are being catered for. It was the network which decided to demand equal access to training courses already available rather than seek women-only courses.

Jenny Groves regards herself as a bit of a thorn in Boots' side. She fought hard to have term-time contracts for pharmacists extended to her area in Essex - and eighteen months ago she won: 'It's been the happiest eighteen months I've spent for years - it's almost perfect.'

She has two sons, aged 10 and 13, and works a twenty-six hour week during the term and Saturdays during the school holidays.

She joined in 1974 to be trained as a pharmacist, and left to have children eighteen months later. She has been part-time ever since – beginning with two hours on a Saturday. She first read about Boots providing term-time working in *New Woman* magazine: at that time she was working on Saturdays, with extra hours, such as lunchtime cover, on an *ad hoc* basis during the week, so she had no job security, and did not find the arrangement satisfactory. At first she was told term-time working did not apply to her area, but finally worked out the contract she wanted.

She believes that this sort of arrangement is in Boots' ultimate interest: 'About 50 per cent of graduates who go into pharmacy are women – 90 per cent will want to take a break of some kind to do something, not necessarily having children. Boots invests an enormous amount of time and money in training and cannot afford to lose all of them. Now they are even considering a proper training scheme for pharmacists returning to work.'

She also believes women are more likely to stay as pharmacists because: 'The further up you go the further away you get from customers and dispensing, which is the best part of the job and why they wanted to be one in the first place.'

She says being a pioneer has been fun: 'It hasn't half made a difference. Not just the job – but the amount of clout it's got me. I've gone from being a non-existent person to somebody to whom people go for advice.'

She believes that more moves will be made to accommodate individual needs as existing schemes are seen to be successful: 'I think the big problem is proving to the company that these things work. I was the first pharmacist on the scheme, when they see it working they will want more. Once you spread the word it's easier and easier to do it.'

She is acting Store Manager as well as being a pharmacist. She has persuaded the company to let her go on management courses – not previously available to part-timers – so that when she goes full-time she can apply for a Store Manager position: 'They can't appoint you as management staff if you work less than thirty hours a week, and I take far too much leave. But now if a job of Manager came up I could go for it and I would go full-time for that.'

In fact, now she need not go full-time to become a Store

Manager, because the Personnel Department would like to initiate a jobshare in store management, but so far no suitable sharers have been found.

Boots is always looking for ways to improve working conditions, particularly to make it easier for people with domestic commitments to work and progress in the company. Heather Clark, a Senior Personnel Officer, says that far from being a thorn in her side Jenny Groves has had a valuable input into company policy: 'She has had a lot of ideas about jobsharing and we have been able to bounce ideas off her. It's good to have such enthusiasm, then we know people are interested.'

*The Littlewoods Organisation was originally created as a
football pools firm in Liverpool. The head office is still in
Liverpool, but the company has expanded to include retail
stores, a mail order business, a print company and a
financial services division. There are 116 chain stores and
ninety-six branches of the Index catalogue shop. The annual
turnover of the organisation exceeds £2 billion. Littlewoods
employs 30,000 people, of whom 10,000 are in based in the
north-west of England. Just over 80 per cent of the workforce
are women.*

Littlewoods

Equal Opps Policy	✓	Crèche	✗
Equal Opps Recruitment	✓	Career Breaks	✓
Monitoring	✓	Jobshares	✓
Positive Action	✓	Flexible Hours	✓

Littlewoods sees itself as having been a pioneer in equal
opportunities over a period of nearly twenty-five years. In 1967,
the organisation examined race discrimination within itself and
became the first company in the private sector to introduce
targets. In the 1980s, the policy was extended to cover gender and
disability.

The company believes that for an equal opportunity policy to be
effective it must be seen to be supported at the very top. The
company's equal opportunity committee is, therefore, chaired by
John Moores, son of the founder of the company and a member
of the Group Board of Directors. Littlewoods does not hesitate to
hammer home the message that equal opportunities is good for
business: using people's abilities to the full, drawing from the
widest possible pool of talent and implementing good management
practice.

The theory is clear: strong leadership at boardroom level, well briefed and motivated senior and middle management, and strongly defined channels of communication ensure that all employees are aware of policies and their effect on individuals. This combination gives everyone a sense of involvement.

Littlewoods learned from the length of time it took their race policies to start working that good intentions are not enough. The firm has changed selection and recruitment policies, introduced good practice in training and has set targets for the promotion of women in the company. Since the introduction of the equal opportunities programme, the proportion of women has increased at all levels of management, so that they now make up 50 per cent of people in management.

Janette Fiddaman is the Training Manager in the Home Shopping Division. She is involved in equal opportunities training and is given the support to do this. However, it is not an easy task. Ms Fiddaman initially joined the Chain Store Division when she started with the company and has done well within Littlewoods, with five moves in five years, each one representing a step up in her career.

While she acknowledges that great gains have been made for women in the company, she says there is still room for improvement: 'There are more and more women senior managers, but in certain areas it is still difficult for women to be taken seriously by men.'

However, she believes it is easier to see flaws when looking from the inside: 'I would find it difficult to go to another company without a high-profile equal opportunities policy. Some other companies are still in the Dark Ages and appear to be either oblivious to equal opportunities legislation or simply behind the times.'

One policy change which has made a big difference within the Chain Store Division is that managers no longer have to be prepared to move all over the UK – the country is now split into areas. Ms Fiddaman has also benefited from the fact that Littlewoods is based in the North-west and that is the geographical area she would prefer to stay in.

The company is also very keen on education, training and development of women in the workforce. There is a well-founded belief that training helps women to be promoted. Pek Har Tan had been a medical secretary when she joined Littlewoods four years ago and was immediately appointed to be a Director's secretary. She has been encouraged to stretch herself: the company paid for her to attend evening classes and get a qualification in business and finance. She is now looking for promotion into marketing – confident that the size of the company will ensure that a place is found for her. Her previous years in the NHS had led her to expect nothing more than a secretarial career.

Very few of the senior women in Littlewoods have children – it is still difficult to mix family and career. Recognising this, Littlewoods has introduced jobsharing, part-time employment and career breaks, and is investigating childcare provision. The company is making sure these conditions apply to all staff, not just the high-flyers. Maternity benefits have been opened up to more women by reducing the qualifying time which entitles them to maternity pay. The paternity leave has been doubled and staff adopting children are entitled to the same benefits.

Littlewoods has targets for women in management at all grades. This was introduced as part of a five-year action programme in 1986. They have been so successful that the target of 20 per cent in middle management was reached by 1990 – one year ahead of schedule – and this has subsequently been revised up to 35 per cent.

It is all slowly working. As John Moores said in the *Equal Opportunities Review*: 'Although the company has made lots of mistakes we have learnt from every single one of them. But perhaps our biggest mistake was to think that the process of implementing change would be simple, whereas it is, in fact, at least a 20 year job for a team. But nobody ever talks about how long it takes.'

Any woman joining Littlewoods can be certain that equal opportunities is taken seriously, and although the battle is far from won at least nobody is being complacent.

Marks & Spencer has 62,00 employees, 52,000 of whom are women, at over 280 stores in the UK, their head offices in Baker Street, London, and substantial retailing interests in Europe, Canada and the Far East. In the USA, they now own Brook Brothers and Kings Supermarkets.

Marks & Spencer

Equal Opps Policy	✓	Crèche	✗
Equal Opps Recruitment	✓	Career Breaks	✓
Monitoring	✓	Jobshares	✓
Positive Action	✗	Flexible Hours	✓

Marks & Spencer is seen as something of an institution: for the customer it is a by-word for value for money; the employees used to bask in the knowledge of working for the cream of the retailing sector. However, while Marks & Spencer still lays claim to the best salaries and benefits package in this country, the competition for good staff has led other stores to vie for the top position.

Marks & Spencer does offer a superb benefits package with profit sharing, subsidised meals, subsidised hairdressing, a Christmas bonus of four weeks salary to all non-management staff, and discount tokens which are issued twice a year and are worth 20 per cent off £1,000-worth of merchandise. Its comprehensive health service includes oral health screening, medical advice, chiropody screening, breast screening and cervical cytology.

Penny Smoker began with Marks & Spencer seventeen years ago when she found herself alone with two children to support. She joined as a temporary seasonal Sales Assistant in Derby and was taken on permanently after the Christmas rush and January sales. She says promotion was easy: 'I think the company does recognise people's potential.' She was an Assistant Administration Manager when she left Derby and is now a Personnel Assistant to one of the Personnel Managers in the company's number one store in London's Marble Arch. She lives in Eastbourne and would not even consider moving to a more convenient store, let alone a different company: 'It's worth travelling seventy-six miles for – and being away from home fourteen hours a day – because I love my job.'

Mercedes Garcia is one of the company's many part-time Sales Assistants. She also works in Marble Arch. She works from 12 a.m. to 6 p.m. four days a week and her husband works on night shifts, so between them they can look after 3-year-old Sebastian. She says that when Sebastian goes to school she will probably change to full-time work but for the moment she is happy: 'I want to stay as a Sales Assistant. I love the job and I love meeting people from all over the world.' Sensibly, the management use her fluent Spanish whenever translation is needed, so she is also able to make use of being bilingual.

Some management women at Marks & Spencer also work part-time. It is a trend spreading through management levels, particularly among women who find it impossible to bring up a child and do a full-time job. Janice Hards is a Press Officer working two days a week – she spends the rest of the time with 3-year-old Rosie. She had worked for Mark & Spencer for fourteen years until the birth of her daughter, joining after a business studies course at college. She originally went back full-time after taking six months off on maternity leave: 'I did it for about a year and a quarter, but I felt I was missing out on an awful lot of her growing up, and I was not happy with myself five days a week. When I was offered the opportunity to go part-time it was up to me to say what I wanted. Originally, I was a jobshare but my partner was pregnant and went off to have twins.'

She views her career as being on hold until she decides to come back full-time. While it is possible for part-time women to be promoted, particularly to take up jobshare positions, not being full-time certainly slows progress down.

If Ms Hards were to have another baby, she could take advantage of the company's new career break scheme for management, which gives up to five years off with a guarantee of coming back at the same level, if not the same job. The scheme is flexible so people can come back and work part-time if they want to. Mothers have an extra incentive for returning full-time – if they do so within four months, they receive full pay throughout their maternity leave.

Samantha Price, a Corporate Press Officer, says crèches or childcare vouchers are not offered because the high percentage of part-time work means that women tend to agree working hours with personnel, and this allows them to organise their domestic lives accordingly. However, the firm is open to reviewing the decision if circumstances change.

Marks & Spencer is so keen to emphasise its care for all employees, rather than any particular group, that one could mistakenly assume that a serious drive for equal opportunities for women has rather fallen by the wayside. In fact, there have been enormous changes in recent years, affecting the entry of women into management and their progress to the top. Personnel policies, therefore, seem to be working. While only 5 per cent of Store Managers are currently women, half of those coming through the system are women, so the numbers should change dramatically.

Donna Bellingham is one of those women coming through the system. She has been with Marks & Spencer for two years, joining their graduate management scheme straight from university. She is now Assistant Manager of the food department in London's Kensington branch: 'I've found promotion is as rapid as I merit. I have not found any hold backs being a woman; if anything, I have been promoted before my male colleagues. I have had three moves, Wolverhampton, Reading and now here, in two years, but I don't really mind moving about. I'll move on again in another six months or so, because junior management appointments tend to last twelve to eighteen months.'

She believes she has chosen the best retail management course in the country: 'It's hard work but very rewarding. I like to work at a pace and thinking on my feet. It's thoroughly enjoyable.'

Penny Smoker says that in the last few years: 'There has been a tremendous change, and stores have changed enormously. Women are there.' Samantha Price says: 'In the eight years that I have been here, I've seen a revolution in the attitude to management, mobility and maternity.'

One change which has particularly benefited women is that management personnel no longer have to be prepared to move anywhere in the country. Although total mobility for most management personnel is an employment requirement, there is a more understanding approach to individuals who want to limit their mobility for domestic reasons.

At a time when conditions for women, particularly working mothers, are being seriously considered by all progressive retailers, it is good that Marks & Spencer is not content to sit on its laurels, but is keeping itself in the forefront of good employment practices.

Sainsbury's has supermarkets throughout the UK and owns Savacentre and Homebase. It has 87,000 employees: 77,000 working for the supermarket chain and 10,000 for Savacentre and Homebase. Two-thirds of its employees are women.

Sainsbury's

Equal Opps Policy	✓	Crèche	✓
Equal Opps Recruitment	✓	Career Breaks	✓
Monitoring	✓	Jobshares	✓
Positive Action	✗	Flexible Hours	✓

Sainsbury's is working hard to be one of the best employers of women in the UK. It is also trying to implement measures that do not just help high-flying women but ensure that good working conditions and chances of promotion exist throughout the company, so people can work their way up from the check-out desks to be a Section Manager of a store and then up the hierarchy.

Six hundred A level students and 200 graduates join Sainsbury's each year, but many more people with little or no formal qualifications are recruited. Jenni Lowden started at Sainsbury's as a temporary cashier while she was still at school. At 17 she had intended to go into the Civil Service but instead she accepted the offer of a job as a Supervisor at Sainsbury's: 'My parents were horrified, they didn't want me sitting at a supermarket till all day.'

She says getting off the shop floor is tough for women because a lot of the work takes physical strength, which means that men tend to progress faster. However, she has been on two training courses, each lasting a year, and is now the Administration Manager of the Streatham Common store in south London.

The ability to progress from the checkout and up the hierarchy has been helped by a new branch management structure that was started in 1988. This reduced the working week from forty-four hours to thirty-nine hours, and increased the number of deputies

from one to three. It instituted the junior management position
of Section Manager, which is the bridge between the shop floor
and management, so that people from the shop floor can have a
career. All Section Managers were allowed to work part-time.
These changes made the whole management structure of the store
more flexible, and work and leisure time more predictable, giving
people regular hours off.

For graduates the path up to management is quicker and more
certain. High-flyer Jane Taylor joined in 1985, and by 1990 was
Deputy Manager at the new Superstore in Chippenham. She is
still in her twenties: 'It's brilliant here. I like to be busy all the
time – I don't like predictable situations. I try to plan but each day
is completely different. As a company there are good
opportunities and the training is excellent.'

She says her gender has never been a problem: 'I've gone up
very fast, overtaking many men. Though as a female it does help
if you stand your ground. For women who want to stay in junior
management it's fine, but for the level I want to achieve it's
tougher for women: I want to get to the top. Already my level in
Sainsbury's is very male dominated.'

Ms Taylor also commends Sainsbury's for not demanding long
hours: 'If I wanted to do thirty-nine hours I could. Sometimes I
work late, sometimes I work on a Sunday; but I do not expect to
do regular long hours. I have a very good and active social life, if
any job stopped me from having a social life I would have to
rethink it.'

Ms Taylor is one of a growing number of women managers and
deputies in Sainsbury's supermarkets: in 1986 there were four;
this figure rose to sixty-nine in 1990. In 1990, almost one-third of
all managers were women.

One important advantage Sainsbury's has as an employer over
many other national retailing outlets is that staff are not expected
to move round the country in order to progress – a twenty-five
mile radius is the rule, which is one of the reasons Jenni Lowden
wants to stay with the company. Jane Taylor says: 'The
opportunities are better if you're prepared to move anywhere, but
I could stay in this area and still progress.'

Both Ms Taylor and Ms Lowden cite the flexibility given to

mothers as a reason for wanting to make their long-term careers
with Sainsbury's. As Danielle Douglas, Employee Relations
Manager responsible for Equal Opportunities, says: 'We have so
many mothers working for us we must take their needs into
account.'

The career break – or bridging scheme as it is called – was
launched in 1989. Originally, it applied only to women in
management, but it has since been widened to include all staff.
The break is for up to five years with an option to return part-time.
It is open to all staff who need time off to look after their children,
and one man has already been accepted on the scheme. Danielle
Douglas is very enthusiastic about it: 'We are offering real
flexibility, trying to design jobs to fit around the needs of the
people. The company is big enough to do this. Of course, there have
been a few teething problems, but we're certain it can be sorted
out. Most of the women look at it in responsible terms and try to
be flexible to make it work.'

There is also a crèche in Sainsbury's Streatham Common store
in London. This is a pilot scheme with thirty places – there are
ten for Sainsbury's employees – which is run with West Lambeth
Health Authority. Jayne Rismanchi's daughter is in the crèche,
and this enabled her to return to work after the birth: 'I used to
work at the Purley Way store and was offered a vacancy here
because of the crèche. I'm one of the few who have had a baby and
managed to come back to work.

'It's brilliant having her in a workplace nursery. I used to pop
in during the lunch break, but I found she was fine and I was upset.
She loves it: they're extremely good and she gets used to different
ethnic groups and religions. She's five minutes away and I feel a
very lucky lady.'

Ms Rismanchi is the Personnel Manager at the Streatham
Common store and finds the nursery has made her restrict her
hours: 'My times are set here but I come in an hour before and
leave an hour later. That's my discipline, because being personnel
in retail is an "open all hours" job as the staff work different shifts.
I would work longer if I didn't have to get her out of the nursery
because I'm a very loyal person and do the job to the best of my
ability.'

Sainsbury's is piloting two other initiatives for parents: childcare vouchers and term-time working. Each store now has a database of women who have left to have children, so they can keep them informed of the jobs available.

The company has a positive policy of retaining older workers in its workforce and attracting those who are nearing or have already reached state retirement age. Danielle Douglas says: 'The company has always aimed to have a mix of older and younger staff since they bring different qualities to their work. Older people have the experience and maturity which helps them relate well to customers. The majority of people over pension age prefer to work restricted hours.'

All this sounds positive, but it is rather diminished by a glance at the page in the *Annual Report and Accounts* showing pictures of the Board of Directors. Right at the bottom is the only woman, Diana Eccles, and she is a non-executive member, even though two-thirds of Sainsbury's employees are women. However, as Danielle Douglas says: 'Equal opportunities is not entirely altruistic. It is to do with resourcing the business; but this is an opportunity for women's careers never to be the same again. After all, why let all this potential lie dormant?'

VOLUNTARY ORGANISATIONS

Oxfam is a Third World charity with its headquarters in Oxford. There are regional offices throughout the UK, and Oxfam shops in almost every town and city in the country. Oxfam emphasises its projects throughout the Third World, encouraging communities to become self-supporting. It also campaigns in the UK to eradicate the roots of poverty, such as Third World debt.

Oxfam

Equal Opps Policy	✓	Crèche	✓
Equal Opps Recruitment	✓	Career Breaks	✗
Monitoring	✓	Jobshares	✓
Positive Action	✗	Flexible Hours	✓

Almost two-thirds of Oxfam's 1,179 staff in Britain are women. They are people who have joined the charity because they believe in its aims rather than for the money, because the salaries are generally low. They expect to see justice for the workforce at home as well as fighting for the rights of those who are taking part in Oxfam projects abroad. For an organisation of such low resources, a lot of effort has been put into equal opportunities.

Undeniably the organisation is male dominated at the top, but this is slowly changing as 35 per cent of senior management and almost half of total management staff, are women. The measures that have been introduced to encourage mothers to return to work after having babies include enhanced maternity pay, a crèche, childcare allowances, jobsharing and flexible hours.

Belinda Coote, a Researcher/Policy Advisor in the Public Affairs Unit, who has a 2½-year-old girl, Bernadette, says being given a place in the crèche is a major reason for her still being with the charity: 'I went back to work when Bernadette was six months old and found it relatively easy to slot back in, with her in the crèche. There is a tremendous psychological, and practical, advantage to having your child in the same building as you, especially when they are young. She is, and always has been, extremely happy there and I would certainly think twice about disrupting that by changing jobs.'

Ms Coote may have returned to full-time work but the hours are far more regulated than before: 'I now work 9 a.m. to 5 p.m. which is a new experience. The Head of Department also has a young child in the crèche. Before we had our children, we both worked much longer hours and often at weekends. Now, the office empties at 5 and we all know nobody will get any work done in the evenings because we are all putting our monsters to bed. To work at a weekend is exceptional. Work is now more civilised. Being a working mother certainly concentrates the mind. You have to be far more efficient and effective with the time that you have. It's tough especially when you are short of sleep – an occupational hazard of motherhood. I am lucky to have an understanding boss. A lot of women in Oxfam don't.

'In my job, I have to travel but I do it much less. Before I had Bernadette I considered this to be a perk. It is an interesting part of the job, but turning down conferences in exotic places is not too much of a sacrifice. I went on one three-week trip and made arrangements so that Bernadette did not suffer. It was agony leaving her, but enormously helpful to both of us to have the continuity of the crèche.'

Louise Douglas is a single mother like Belinda Coote, but she has three children. She began working for Oxfam as the South-west Education Worker based in Bristol, covering for a woman on maternity leave. When the woman decided not to go back full-time at the end of her maternity leave, Ms Douglas teamed up with her for a jobshare. She is now on maternity leave again. Ms Douglas is happy either way: 'A permanent jobshare suits me, but financially I would rather be full-time.

'Oxfam is sympathetic to children and I have always made it clear my children come first. I am expected to go to Oxford for meetings which might last a couple of days, but I always come back rather than stay the night. My Head of Department says children come before jobs. If they are sick I take the day off.'

Dorothy Clark has worked her way up to managing Oxfam's shop in Coventry, starting as a volunteer on Saturday afternoons eleven years ago. With four children, she decided to begin slowly and gradually she increased her hours until she was made Shop Leader three years ago, on five half-days a week.

She is happy to make it the peak of her career: 'I really enjoy it here. As long as I can stay in Coventry I'm happy to stay with Oxfam and I will continue as long as I can.'

In the six years that Belinda Coote has worked for Oxfam she has noticed an increase in the number of women in senior management jobs, but she observes: 'The women who get to senior management posts in Oxfam tend to be extremely capable, probably a great deal more so than their male counterparts. But you don't see many who are trying to bring up children. Oxfam puts extraordinary demands on its managers which in reality excludes people who can't or don't wish to be endlessly flexible and generous with their time – such as the vast majority of working mothers. It means that a lot of women, like myself, would never even consider moving beyond a certain point in the Oxfam career hierarchy. I think that this is a tremendous organisational weakness.'

The women who work for Oxfam appear more critical of the organisation than many would be in commercial companies, probably because they have higher expectations of the charity, rather than because of its lower standards. Belinda Coote says: 'They have gone part of the way but Oxfam has a long way to go before going the whole way. It has got to be more realistic.' Louise Douglas adds: 'My feeling is that Oxfam tries very hard to be an equal opportunities employer, but it is difficult to achieve genuine equal opportunities. Oxfam is not completely there but neither is it failing.

'The organisation has a philosophy and beliefs and has to put them into practice. Being a woman I believe strongly in working for an organisation which tries to put that into practice. It is very important.'

Oxfam does a lot for working mothers, in making it possible to mix a career and family, but as long as it has a long-hours culture, where the time put into the organisation is seen as the level of commitment to it, it will be impossible for many women to achieve their potential, and the charity will continue to be staffed at the top by men.

Save The Children Fund is the largest international children's charity in the UK, working with children in both this country and abroad. The headquarters are in south London, with nine divisional offices and one hundred project sites spread across the UK. Save The Children employs 730 people in the UK, 557 of whom are women.

Save The Children Fund

Equal Opps Policy	✓	Crèche	✗
Equal Opps Recruitment	✓	Career Breaks	✗
Monitoring	✓	Jobshares	✓
Positive Action	✓	Flexible Hours	✓

Save The Children has three separate working groups looking at the promotion of equal opportunities across the organisation. They concentrate on employment practice, UK fieldwork practice and public image and media presentation; a sub-group of the Employment Practice Group has been set up specifically to look at possible positive action on gender issues. With policies which make it easier for mothers to work and which have overhauled the recruitment process already in place, many organisations would be content to sit on their laurels. However, for Save The Children, equal opportunities means continually looking at how the organisation works to improve itself.

Kate Harper, a Childminding Adviser in Manchester, who is the Chairperson of all the union representatives in the charity, has been one of the agitators for change. She is full of compliments: 'It's a good employer – there are good terms and conditions for the staff and the charity has a positive attitude in trying to develop good practice.'

She is a single parent of teenagers and joined five years ago when reduced childcare commitments finally allowed her to work full-time: 'I had been for quite a few interviews which had been unpleasant. At one for a job with a union, I was asked how I could cope with work and childcare responsibilities. Needless to say I did not get the job. When I came here neither my status nor my children were mentioned. However, when I got my job, my boss told me that if I worked a late night she did not expect to see me on time the next day so I could see the children. She also said he did not want me to be tired out.

'I have always felt there is a lot of flexibility here, and it works very well. If you are treated fairly, you will be fair to them and work quite hard.'

Ms Harper still believes there is a long way to go: 'The union, Manufacturing Science and Finance, has done research with the UK staff on the needs of staff and dependents. We are looking at negotiating a dependents' package.' A proposal is also being put forward to extend the paid maternity leave. Currently, staff can have up to a year off, but only four months of that is paid. The Save The Children Fund is reviewing the maternity policy, as well as considering career breaks and waiving the two-year qualification for maternity benefits. The organisation has already introduced a dependent care allowance scheme for staff.

Leonie Lonton, who is now the Overseas Personnel Manager, worked in UK Personnel when she had Hannah, who is now 2. She took four months off and then came back three days a week for the first month, and four days a week for the second. She found her return much easier than she had thought: 'Largely because people were incredibly thoughtful and sensitive.' She ran two residential courses during her leave. They worked well but she was still breastfeeding, and although the baby at home had bottles of stored expressed milk, she had to keep excusing herself from the course to express the overflow that she was still producing.

Ms Lonton applied for her current job, which not only entailed promotion but also overseas travel, after her return. She has negotiated the overseas travel down to a month a year in two trips, which she finds easier to accommodate than the many odd nights away that her previous job involved: 'At least I can plan for it. Previously, I could be made to go to Belfast or Scotland for a meeting at very little notice.'

She believes the key to a more fundamental change is coming

now that men are acknowledging that they want more to do with the family: 'Once men make demands it will change the whole climate.'

The Fund has jobsharing and various other flexible working arrangements. It has also made what appear to be smaller changes, but these can be just as important as the larger ones. Training courses are organised to start at 10 or 11 a.m., instead of 9 a.m., so people with outside commitments do not have to be away from their homes the night before. And there is leave for looking after sick children.

Ms Lonton says that, in her ten years with the Fund, it has changed enormously, partly because of the professionalisation of the voluntary sector: 'For example, the fundraising field force used to recruit predominantly second career people, i.e. male ex-police or army officers. Now these are acknowledged to be challenging jobs requiring recognised skills, and are particularly good for women because you have control of your diary and work from home.'

She acknowledges that problems do exist in promotion, because there is a bottleneck to get into senior management, with many able people and few posts to give them. Women, however, do make up 45 per cent of senior management, 63 per cent of management overall and 87 per cent of staff outside management. With so much talent and potential available within the organisation, the Fund has recognised that there needs to be a focus on internal career development opportunities as well as external recruitment strategies.

What is refreshing about Save The Children is the continuing thought that goes into planning equal opportunities. Ms Lonton says there are two main reasons why the charity has a good track record. One is that 'the place is full of competent, strong women'. The other is 'the area in which we are working: the link between being a good practitioner and a good employer, both of which should be based on the principles embodied in the Save The Children charter of the rights of the child'.

Ms Harper sums up the irony of charities trying to institute good employment policy, which of course costs money: 'The problem is that people donating to a charity might not expect it to go on staffing needs. However, I believe if you employ good, qualified staff and spend money on provision, it is more likely the staff will stay. It is economically viable for any charity to retain staff.'

The Save The Children Fund demonstrates just what a charity with limited resources can achieve for its women employees.

PART 3

HONOURABLE MENTIONS

Abbey National: Recruitment policy has been overhauled to come into line with the rest of the equal opportunity policy. Career breaks and improvements to the maternity provisions are being considered. Part-time work is offered to all women returners where possible.

Air UK: Jobsharing.

Allied Dunbar: There is a workplace nursery. A childminding network is being established. Career breaks, jobshares and other flexible hours arrangements are under consideration. Pensions and company cars are kept during maternity leave.

Allied Irish Bank: Has produced a brochure on employment equality.

Amersham International: 12 months qualification for maternity leave. 13 weeks at 100 per cent normal pay, one month dependent on return to work for 3 months. Jobsharing on return from maternity leave or part-time or reduced hours.

Aquascutum: Workplace nursery in Milton Keynes and Kettering.

Asda: Maternity leave after one year of service. Sexual harassment policy.

Bank of England: Has equal opportunity training for all staff and open performance assessment systems which should ensure women with potential are promoted. Career breaks are available.

Bank of Ireland: Offers a career break for childcare or other reasons, for instance study or travel.

Bass: Part-time or reduced hours on return from maternity leave.

Birmingham City Council: Jobsharing.

Bournemouth Borough Council: Nursery.

Bowyers (Wiltshire) Ltd: 6 months qualification for maternity leave. Female managers and supervisors entitled to full pay if only off for 3 months. Workplace nursery.

Brighton Borough Council: Workplace nursery. No maternity qualification.

Bristol City Council: Many women-only training courses. Maternity leave up to 52 weeks with 12 weeks on half pay plus lower rate standard maternity pay with no obligation to return to work. All posts open to jobsharing. Flexible hours on department by department basis.

British Airways: Offer separate training courses for women.

British Bata Shoe Co: Revised recruitment application form.

British Gas: Jobsharing. One year maternity qualification. Maternity pay: 6 weeks at 90 per cent plus 12 weeks half pay if return to work for 3 months. Consider return after maternity leave on part-time basis. All benefits maintained during maternity leave. Career break started 1988: up to 2 years. Pensions: widowers paid out to. Decade of retirement 55-65. Positive action: encouragement of recruitment of women especially into engineering-type jobs; training courses for women.

British Waterways: Jobsharing or part-time work after maternity leave at management's discretion.

Buckinghamshire County Council: Nursery. Career breaks. Part-time work. Flexi-time.

Burton Group Plc: Right to return after maternity leave after one year's service.

Cabot Carbon: Jobsharing. Maternity pay 9 weeks at 100 per cent not dependent on return.

Clerical Medical and General Life Assurance Society: Mortgage subsidy kept during maternity leave. A lot of part-time working and some home working. Most staff on flexi-time.

Cookson Group: Jobsharing. Can go part-time on return to work.

Crosfield Electronics: Breast and cervical screening.

Cuprinol: Jobsharing. Reduced hours on return from maternity leave.

Dixons Stores: Term-time working contracts.

Eagle Star Insurance: A job evaluation exercise carried out with the Equal Opportunities Commission to win equal pay for women workers had a direct impact on pay of women workers. Runs short courses aimed at women returners.

East Hertfordshire Health Authority: Jobsharing career break up to 5 years. Part-time, flexible hours, term-time only contracts.

East Suffolk Health Authority Community Nursing: Jobsharing.

Economist Group: 20 weeks full maternity pay. 13 weeks payable on return at new salary if higher. Retain company car during maternity leave.

Eurosearch Ltd: Positive action: women's discussion, self-development groups, confidence building.

Financial Times: Jobsharing.

Ford Motor Company: Signed statement with unions making every employee responsible for implementing equal opportunities. Women in management courses.

Fram Europe: 12 months qualification for maternity leave.

Galleon Roadchef: Right to return from maternity leave after one year's service.

Goldsmith's College (London): Nursery.

Granada TV: One year maternity qualification.

Guide Dogs for the Blind: Women can return on a part-time basis after maternity leave if there is a vacancy, either immediately following maternity leave or within one year of the birth.

Hampshire County Council: Working from home is a part of a package of flexible working arrangements, including jobsharing, annual hours contracts and career break schemes. The council says at least 500 posts have the potential to be done from home.

Harlow Council: Childcare subsidy paid to employees.

Harold Wood Hospital (Romford, Essex): Nursery.

Hay: Part-time or reduced hours on return from maternity leave.

Haymarket Publishing: Adoptive children under 12 months covered by company's maternity and pay arrangements. 5 days paternity leave. Childcare payments.

Hillingdon Hospital: Day nursery.

Holiday Inn: Workplace nurseries at Heathrow and Croydon.

Inmos: Discretionary part-time and reduced hours on return from maternity leave.

Institute of Housing: Career break.

Investors in Industry: On maternity leave pensions continue, car can still be used, but petrol must be paid for, and low mortgage rate continues. Full-time employees are given 4 months full pay for maternity leave, 2 months to be paid on return to work. Some part-time working has been arranged.

IPC Magazines: Fund for childcare costs. 10 days paternity leave.

ITN: Jobsharing. Enhanced maternity leave – 13 weeks full pay.

Jaeger Ladieswear: Part-time or reduced hours on return from maternity leave.

Joint Credit Card: Part-time or reduced hours are available on return from maternity leave. Adoptive parents' leave.

Kalamazoo: Offers separate training courses for women.

Kent County Council: Jobsharing and working from home.

Leeds Building Society: Some women sent on external women-only courses like assertiveness training. Low mortgages and status cars continue during maternity leave. There are career breaks. Jobshares are available to all levels of staff on an *ad hoc* basis as well as part-time and flexi-time.

Leeds City Council: Jobsharing. Maternity leave provides the right to return as jobshare.

Leeds East District Health Authority: Jobsharing.

Life Science Research: Part-time or reduced hours on return from maternity leave.

Link House Advertising Periodicals: 12 months qualification for maternity leave, 18 months for pay. Maternity pay: 13 weeks full pay plus 16 weeks half pay, payable in 3 equal monthly instalments beginning one month after return. Part-time or reduced hours offered on return.

Liverpool Daily Post: Maternity pay for journalists: 12 weeks at 90 per cent dependent on return.

Lloyds Bank: Career break which covers all employees. Staff may opt for part-time working.

Lombard North Central: Overhauled its recruitment procedure. Two residential courses for women – called the Women's Development Programme. Career breaks offered and part-time and flexible hours.

London & Manchester Group: A 16-place day nursery at head office in Exeter, which is heavily subsidised. All benefits are maintained during maternity leave.

London Borough of Camden: Jobsharing. Nursery for employees' children. Must be in permanent employment by confinement to qualify for maternity pay. 16 weeks full pay plus 24 weeks half pay. Must return to work for 2 months if not may be asked to repay any over and above the 16 weeks. Part-time or reduced hours on return.

London Borough of Hackney: Jobsharing. Nursery. Six months qualification for maternity pay. Up to 40 weeks leave and more if baby is late. Pay: 6 weeks at 90 per cent plus 18 weeks at half pay – must return to work to be entitled to the 18 weeks.

London Borough of Southwark: Women-only courses. 30 places in borough nurseries. Career breaks, part-time, flexible working hours, jobsharing.

London Fire and Civil Defence Authority: Childcare allowance for all staff with over 12 months service. Allowance depends on total household income: more income means lower allowance. Limited to under 5s and paid during sick leave but not annual leave.

London Underground Ltd: Women-only training course: women

into management. Campaign to encourage women to seek promotion. Discretionary jobshares, office-based staff entitled to flexi-time.

Lothian Health Board: Jobsharing.

McDonalds: Part-time management scheme for employees with dependent children, other part-time has always been available.

Medelec: Jobsharing. Part-time or reduced hours on return from maternity leave.

Merrill Lynch: Built City Child nursery as planning permission condition from London Borough of Islington. The company has first option on 30 places.

Middlesex Polytechnic: Jobsharing.

Mid Essex Health Authority: Nursery.

Nationwide Anglia: Career break scheme for managers and potential managers. Low mortgage rates maintained during maternity leave for women intending to return.

Next: 12 months maternity qualification.

North Bedfordshire Health Authority: Jobsharing.

Norwich Union: Career break option for all staff. Period of maternity absence counts retrospectively for mortgage allowance and pension purposes, subject to return to work for 6 months. Part-timers working over 20 hours a week have access to mortgage allowance, pension, private health insurance and sick pay benefits on similar basis to full-time staff. Term-time work available.

Oxford University Press: One year maternity qualification. 52 weeks maternity leave. Missed pension contributions during maternity leave may be paid over following two years.

Penguin Books: Jobsharing. Holiday play scheme. 12 months qualification for maternity pay; up to 52 weeks maternity leave. Maternity pay: 25 weeks at full pay but must return to work for 5 months to be entitled to pay above statutory entitlement. 15 days paid leave when children ill for NUJ members. Childcare payments organised by unions represented and contributed to by the employees.

Peter Dominic: Encourage women to be managers.

Phillips Components: Blood pressure and breast screening.

Post Office: Jobsharing or part-time work after maternity leave at management discretion. 12 month qualification for maternity pay. 13 weeks full pay. Woman must return for 13 weeks in order to be entitled to last 5 weeks. Pension: scheme for children of both parents. Training schemes for women executives.

Rank Hovis McDougal (RHM): Part-time or reduced hours on return from maternity leave.

Reading Borough Council: Nursery. Jobsharing plus various reduced hours schemes. Sexual harassment: has comprehensive agreement with unions and since introduction 'numbers and problems reduced dramatically'.

Reed Business Publishing: Childcare welfare scheme. Employer pays lump sum into scheme based on £x per employee, budget increases annually with RPI. Amount depends on claims received. Pre-school children for whom employees make regular payment. One year maternity qualification.

Refuge Assurance: Has a workplace nursery. During the school holidays operates a playscheme for older children.

Rists: Part-time or reduced hours on return from maternity leave.

Rowntree Mackintosh: One year maternity qualification for all staff working over 14½ hours a week.

Royal Assurance: Career break of up to 10 years – this is only open to higher-grade staff with at least 5 years service. Access to scheme by management invitation. Mortgage subsidy paid retrospectively after return from maternity leave. 2 months salary bonus on return to work. Courses on career development for women run by the Industrial Society.

Royal Borough of Kingston upon Thames: Women-only courses run for employees. Running recruitment advertising aimed at women returners. Career break, part-time work, jobsharing and flexi-time scheme all on offer.

Royal National Institute for the Deaf: Offer management training and assertiveness training courses to women.

Rumbelows: After maternity leave, initial return to work on part-time basis possible for some staff.

Runwell Hospital (Southend): Nursery.

Scotrail: Scheme to enable women in traditionally female jobs to enter predominantly male environments.

Scottish & Newcastle Breweries: Maternity pay 6 weeks full pay not dependent on return to work. Part-time or reduced hours on return to work.

Southampton Council: Childcare subsidy paid to employees.

South West Thames Regional Health Authority: Childcare vouchers worth £25 per week per family are available to all staff, full-time or part-time, who have worked for 3 months and have a child under 4.

Sun Life: Equal opportunities recruitment training. Operates a career break scheme. 6 weeks full salary for maternity leave. Flexible working hours with some part-time working.

Sunderland Forge Services: 12 months qualification for maternity leave, 41 weeks allowed. 11 weeks full pay not dependent on return to work.

Target Life (pensions company, Alyesbury): Offering staff 5 places at shared crèche in Aylesbury College.

Thistle Hotels: Term-time contract for women with children at school, mostly at operative levels but might move to supervisory levels.

Thorpe Park Amusements: Workplace nursery.

Time Out: Maternity pay: 6 months full pay if she returns. £40 per week childcare allowance for pre-school children. 6 weeks paternity leave.

Tyne Tees Television: 18 months qualification for maternity pay. 18 weeks full pay not dependent on return to work. Part-time or reduced hours allowed on return from maternity leave.

Unilever: Career break limited to management staff but

subsidiary companies free to adopt scheme for other employee groups as required.

United Biscuits UK Ltd: Career break.

United Dominions Trust: Assertiveness training for women - life planning, career planning, individual and group counselling. Encourages women to cross from clerical to main career routes in sales or computing, also getting men to appreciate the range of often under-valued skills and techniques which women have bought to their jobs.

Victoria Wine: Encourages women to be managers.

Virgin Retail: Part-time or reduced hours on return from maternity leave.

Vis News: 13 weeks full maternity pay.

Warner Lambert: Well woman clinics.

Wellcome Foundation: Senior manager appointed with responsibility for monitoring equal opportunity policy - specifically, pay, recruitment, promotion, transfer and training. Non-job related training for women. Flexible approach to maternity absence, more part-time opportunities for mothers returning to work, assistance with childcare and offer of paternity and parental leave.

West Midlands Regional Health Authority: Jobsharing.

Yorkshire Bank: Career break available.

COMPANIES WHICH HAVE EQUAL OPPORTUNITIES RECRUITMENT

Abbey National
Alliance & Leicester
   Building Society
Allied Carpet Stores Ltd
BBC
BP
Bank of England
Barclays Bank
Boots The Chemist
Bowyers (Wiltshire) Ltd
Bristol City Council
British Aerospace
British Bata Shoe Company
British Council
British Leyland
British Rail
British Telecom
Brown & Root (UK) Ltd
Buckinghamshire County
   Council
Bull HN Information
   Systems Ltd
Cambridge City Council
Channel Four
Clerical Medical & General
   Life Assurance Society
Co-op
Croydon Health Authority

Curry's
Edinburgh District Council
Esso
Eurosearch Ltd
Ford Motor Company
GEC
Glaxo Group
Gloucestershire County
   Council
Gulliver Treatments
Hughes and Salvidge
ICI
Innoxa
John Lewis
Leeds Building Society
Legal & General
Leicester City Council
Lilley Research Centre
Littlewoods
Lombard North Central
London Borough of Hackney
London Borough of
   Islington
London Borough of
   Southwark
London Underground Ltd
London Weekend Television
McDonalds

Marks & Spencer
Mars
Merseyside Drugs Council
Midland Bank
Multiplex Techniques Ltd
NALGO
National Westminster Bank
Oxfam
Oyez
Pizzaland
Prudential Corporation
Reading Borough Council
Rover Group
Royal Bank of Scotland
Royal Borough of Kingston
    Upon Thames

Royal National Institute for
    the Deaf
Sainsbury's
Save The Children Fund
Seesmograph
Sheffield City Council
Shell
W.H. Smith
Sun Life
Sun Life of Canada
Television South West
Thames Television
TSB
Usher and Partners
VAG (United Kingdom) Ltd
Wellcome Foundation

COMPANIES WHICH ARE TAKING ACTION TO GET MORE WOMEN INTO MANAGEMENT OR INTO MALE-DOMINATED TECHNICAL AREAS

BBC: Targets for women into management, production and technical jobs.

British Council: Positive action to encourage women into overseas service.

British Gas: Encouragement of recruitment of women, particularly in engineering jobs.

British Rail: Gender targets for recruitment.

ICI: Management targets for women.

Leicester City Council: Targets for women and ethnic minorities for each department.

Littlewoods: Targets for women in management.

London Borough of Hackney: Equality target of 50 per cent female employment.

London Underground Ltd: Campaign to persuade women to seek promotion.

London Weekend Television: Targets for women in management.

Mars: Targets for women in management.

Scotrail: Scheme to enable women in traditionally female jobs to enter predominantly male environment.

Thames TV: Women only technical training course to get more women into technical areas.

TSB: Target women into management.

COMPANIES WHICH RUN WOMEN-ONLY TRAINING COURSES

BBC: A variety of women-only courses.

Barclays Bank: Career skills development for junior managers.

Bristol City Council: Lots of women-only courses.

British Airways: Separate training courses for women.

British Council: Women in management evenings.

British Gas: Training courses for women.

British Rail: Women's development courses, women management development courses, management skills for women.

Cambridge City Council: Once-a-year assertiveness courses.

Eagle Star Insurance: Courses for women returners.

Edinburgh District Council: 4 courses a year.

Eurosearch Ltd: Women's discussion groups, self-development groups, confidence building groups.

Ford Motor Company: Women in management courses.

Gloucestershire County Council: Effective Career Development for Women one-day course every month.

John Lewis: Retraining schemes for women.

Kalamazoo: Separate training courses for women.

Leeds Building Society: External assertiveness training courses.

Leicester City Council: Some women-only courses.

Lombard North Central: Week-long residential Women's Development Programme twice a year.

London Borough of Hackney: Many women-only courses.

London Borough of Islington: 4 women-only courses annually.

London Borough of Southwark: Many courses, including self-defence, assertiveness and realising potential courses. Some Black women only courses.

London Underground Ltd: Women into management courses.

London Weekend Television: Effectiveness courses twice a year.

Littlewoods: Assertiveness training.

Marks & Spencer: Training schemes for women executives.

Midland Bank: Residential courses held for women and one-day workshops held on regional basis.

Post Office: For women executives.

Prudential Corporation: Residential Career Development for Women course 4 times a year.

Rank Xerox: Separate training courses for women.

Royal Borough of Kingston Upon Thames: 4 women-only courses annually.

Royal Insurance: Courses in career development for women run by the Industrial Society.

Royal National Institute for the Deaf: Management training and assertiveness training for women.

Sheffield City Council: Some departmental training teams run courses, women's management courses run centrally and courses for low-paid women.

Thames Television: Personal development courses twice a year, developing managerial skills for women once a year.

United Dominions Trust: Assertiveness training for women courses.

Wellcome Foundation: Non job-related training.

Yorkshire Television: Presentation and public speaking skills for women, assertiveness for women, personal effectiveness for women courses.

Companies which Provide Health Care

Abbey National: Health checks available to all over 35; staff grade 11 and above 3 yearly medical.

Alliance & Leicester: Health screening and cervical screening by Occupational Health Department in Hove.

BP: Cancer screening.

Bristol City Council: Counselling and training to give up smoking.

British Rail: Well woman clinics.

Buckinghamshire County Council: No smoking policy.

Channel Four: Annual well woman screening.

Crosfield Electronics: Breast and cervical screening.

Debenhams: Full medical check.

Edinburgh District Council: Health care unit offers screening.

Leeds Building Society: No smoking policy. Course run to help give it up. Counsellor for welfare issues.

Legal & General: No smoking policy. Large offices have full-time nurse.

Leicester City Council: No smoking.

Lombard North Central: Occupational Health nurse on the premises.

London Borough of Islington: Smoking ban.

London Borough of Southwark: Cancer screening.

London Weekend Television: Occupational health unit; regular cervical smear and breast checks; no smoking policy, smoking counselling.

Marks & Spencer: Cervical cancer screening; full medical checks.

Ove Arup: Well woman screening. Subsidised habit-breakers courses.

Phillips Components: Blood pressure checks; breast screening.

Prudential Corporation: Occupational health department; well woman clinic.

Reading Borough Council: Cancer screening; alcohol and smoking counselling.

Rover Group: Health screening for all employees.

Royal Bank of Scotland: Cancer screening.

Royal Borough of Kingston Upon Thames: Cancer screening campaign; giving up smoking support group.

Television South West: No smoking policy.

Thames Television: Cancer screening, alcohol counselling.

Yorkshire Television: Well woman screening.

3i: Free annual well woman screening check; annual medical for women over 40.

COMPANIES WITH POLICIES ON SEXUAL HARASSMENT

Asda
Barclays Bank
BP
British Rail
British Telecom
Edinburgh District Council
GEC
Gloucestershire County
   Council
Leicester City Council
Lombard North Central
London Borough of Hackney
London Borough of Islington

London Borough of
   Southwark
London Underground Ltd
London Weekend Television
McDonalds
NALGO
Prudential Corporation
Reading Borough Council
Royal Bank of Scotland
Sheffield City Council
Thames Television
Yorkshire Television

COMPANIES WITH MATERNITY PROVISION ABOVE THE STATUTORY MINIMUM

Amersham International: One year qualification; 13 weeks full pay, one month dependent on return.

Asda: One year qualification.

Bank of England: Qualifying period one year; extra 7 weeks pay 3 months after return to work.

Bowyers (Wiltshire) Ltd: 6-month qualification; full pay if only off work for 3 months for managers and supervisors.

BP: 4 months on full pay.

Brighton Borough Council: No maternity qualification; extended leave.

Bristol City Council: 12 weeks half pay plus lower standard maternity pay; 52 weeks leave.

British Gas: One year qualification; 6 weeks at 90 per cent pay plus 12 weeks half pay if return to work for 3 months.

Brown & Root (UK) Ltd: 26 weeks at 30 per cent pay; 26 weeks at 25 per cent pay with less than 2 years service.

Burton Group: One year qualification for right to return.

Cabot Carbon: 9 weeks full pay not dependent on return.

Cambridge City Council: One year qualification; 26 weeks full pay or 6 weeks full pay and 34 weeks half pay, dependent on return for 6 months.

Channel Four: 18 months qualification; 4 months full pay; one month for those not qualified.

Edinburgh District Council: One year qualification; six weeks at 90 per cent pay, 12 weeks half pay.

Esso: One year qualification; 2 months full pay plus

standard maternity pay; if return within 26 weeks 2 months salary after 3 months.

Fram Europe: One year qualification.

Galleon Roadchef: Right to return after one year's service.

Independent Television News (ITN): 13 weeks pay.

Legal & General: No eligibility criteria; full pay for 18 weeks for managers; 25 per cent salary supplement for staff on return for 6 months; holiday accrued for time off.

Link House Advertising Periodicals: One year qualification for leave, 18 months for pay; 13 weeks on full pay, 16 weeks on half pay.

Littlewoods: One year qualification; same applies to adoptive parents.

Liverpool Daily Post: 12 weeks at 90 per cent dependent on return.

London Borough of Camden: No qualification; 16 weeks full pay plus 24 weeks half pay dependent on return for 2 months.

London Borough of Hackney: 6 months qualification; 6 weeks at 90 per cent pay plus 18 weeks half pay dependent on return.

London Borough of Islington: No qualification period; 90 per cent pay for 6 weeks, full pay for 10 weeks or half pay for 24 weeks dependent on return; 51 weeks off.

London Borough of Southwark: 9 weeks on full pay, 18 weeks on half pay.

London Weekend Television: 18 months qualification; 19 weeks on full pay, 6 dependent on return to work; one year off.

Mars: 40 weeks off, 6 months pay.

NALGO: One year qualification; 8 weeks full pay, 12 half pay; 41 weeks leave.

Next: One year qualification.

Ove Arup: With over 5 years service, maternity pay plus 3 months salary.

Oxford University Press: One year maternity qualification; 52 weeks leave.

Penguin Books: One year qualification; 25 weeks

full pay dependent on return for 5 months.

Post Office: One year qualification; 13 weeks full pay, last 5 dependent on return for 3 months.

Reading Borough Council: One year qualification; 63 weeks leave.

Reed Business Publications: One year qualification

Research Development Services: 40 per cent pay for 4 months.

Rover Group: One year qualification; 6 weeks on full pay.

Royal Insurance: One year qualification; 2 month salary bonus on return to work.

Scottish & Newcastle Breweries: 6 weeks full pay.

Sheffield City Council: One year qualification; 12 weeks full pay plus 12 weeks half pay if return to work.

Shell: 6 months on full pay.

Sun Life: 6 weeks full pay.

Sunderland Forge Services: One year qualification; 11 weeks full pay not dependent on return; 41 weeks off.

Television South West: 13 weeks full pay.

Thames Television: 12 months qualification; 13 weeks full pay.

Time Out: 6 months full pay.

Tyne Tees Television: 18 month qualification; 18 weeks full pay not dependent on return to work.

Vis News: 13 weeks full pay.

Yorkshire Television: 13 weeks full pay plus five weeks standard maternity pay.

3i: 4 months full pay, 2 to be paid on return to work for full-time employees.

COMPANIES WITH CHILDCARE PROVISION

Allied Dunbar: Workplace nursery.

Aquascutum: Nursery.

BBC: Nurseries.

Bournemouth Borough Council: Nursery.

Bowyers (Wiltshire) Ltd: Nursery.

Brighton Borough Council: Nursery.

British Aerospace: Nursery at Warton site.

Channel Four: £100 per week for mothers with children under 14.

City Limits: Childcare payments; 20 weeks parental leave.

GEC: Nursery.

Goldsmith's College (London): Nursery.

Harlow Council: Childcare subsidy paid to employees.

Haymarket Publishing: Childcare payments.

Hillingdon Hospital: Day nursery.

Holiday Inn: Nurseries at Heathrow and Croydon.

IPC Magazines: Fund for childcare costs.

Leicester City Council: Nursery.

London and Manchester Group: Nursery.

London Borough of Camden: Nursery.

London Borough of Hackney: 2 nurseries.

London Borough of Islington: 2 nurseries.

London Borough of Southwark: 30 places in borough nurseries.

London Fire and Civil Defence Authority: Childcare allowance.

London Weekend Television: Places in 2 local nurseries.

Mars: Places in local nursery.

Merrill Lynch: Built nursery as part of planning condition from Islington Council; first option on 30 places.

Mid Essex Health Authority: Nursery.

Midland Bank: Programme for 300 nurseries.

NALGO: Nursery.

Oxfam: Nursery.

Oxford County Council: Nursery.

Penguin Books: Fund for childcare costs, organised and paid for by 3 unions represented.

Prudential Corporation: Nursery.

Reading Borough Council: Nursery.

Reed Business Publishing: Childcare payments for pre-school children.

Refuge Assurance: Nursery.

Rover Group: Nursery and provision of childminding agencies.

Runwell Hospital (Southend): Nursery.

Sainsbury's: Nursery plus pilot scheme of childcare vouchers.

Southampton Council: Childcare subsidy paid to employees.

TSB: Nursery at Birmingham head office, 1992.

Target Life: 5 places in shared nursery with Aylesbury College.

Thames Television: Places in nursery and childcare allowance.

Thorpe Park Amusements: Nursery.

Time Out: £40 per week childcare allowance.

Trade Union Congress: Places in nursery.

COMPANIES WITH FLEXIBLE HOURS AND CONDITIONS ON RETURN FROM MATERNITY LEAVE

Abbey National: Part-time work offered where possible to returners.

Air UK: Jobsharing.

Alliance & Leicester: Career breaks, jobshares and other part-time arrangements.

Amersham International: Jobsharing, part-time and reduced hours.

BBC: Career breaks, jobsharing, reduced hours.

BP: Career break, jobsharing and part-time.

Bank of England: Career break.

Barclays Bank: Career breaks with part-time options.

Bass: Part-time or reduced hours for returners.

Birmingham City Council: Jobsharing.

Boots The Chemist: Career breaks, jobshares, term-time working.

Bristol City Council: Jobsharing available for all posts; flexible working hours up to individual departments.

British Aerospace: Career breaks, part-time working, term-time working.

British Gas: Career breaks, jobsharing, some part-time for returners.

British Rail: Career break, jobsharing, part-time working, term-time working.

British Telecom: Career break, jobsharing, some homeworking.

British Waterways: Jobsharing and part-time work at management discretion.

Brown & Root (UK) Ltd: Flexible hours, jobsharing, term-time contracts.

Bull HN Information Systems Ltd: Career breaks, jobshares, flexible hours.

Cabot Carbon: Jobsharing.

Cambridge City Council: Career breaks, jobsharing, flexi-time, some term-time working and working from home.

Channel Four: Some flexible working.

Clerical Medical & General Life Assurance: Part-time, evening and Saturday shifts, flexi-time, some homeworking.

Cookson Group: Jobsharing, can go part-time on return to work.

Croydon Health Authority: Career breaks, jobsharing, plus assortment of reduced hours contracts.

Cuprinol: Jobsharing, reduced hours for returners.

Dixons: Term-time working contracts.

East Hertfordshire Health Authority: Career break, jobsharing, part-time, flexible hours, term-time contracts.

East Suffolk Health Authority Community Nursing: Jobsharing.

Edinburgh District Council: Jobsharing, part-time work and flexible hours.

Esso: Career breaks, jobsharing, part-time work.

GEC: Some career breaks and flexi-time.

Gloucestershire County Council: Jobsharing, widespread part-time working, flexi-time, term-time working.

Guide Dogs For The Blind: Part-time for returners if job available.

Hampshire County Council: Career breaks, term-time working, jobsharing, annual hours contracts.

ICI: Career breaks, flexible hours.

Inmos: Discretionary part-time or reduced hours for returners.

Institute of Housing: Career breaks.

Jaeger Ladieswear: Part-time or reduced hours for returners.

John Lewis: Term-time only contracts in Waitrose.

Joint Credit Card: Part-time or reduced hours available for returners.

Leeds Building Society: Career breaks, jobsharing, part-time, flexi-time.

Leeds City Council: Jobsharing.

Leeds East District Health Authority: Jobsharing.

Legal & General: Career break, jobsharing, flexi-time, annual hours contracts, part-time work.

Leicester City Council: Career break, jobsharing, flexi-time, piloting homeworking.

Life Science Research: Part-time or reduced hours for returners.

Littlewoods: Part-time or reduced hours for returners.

Lombard North Central: Career breaks, jobsharing, flexi-time.

London Borough of Camden: Jobsharing, part-time work or reduced hours for returners.

London Borough of Hackney: Jobsharing, flexi-time.

London Borough of Islington: Jobsharing and part-time work.

London Borough of Southwark: Career break, part-time flexible working hours, jobsharing.

London Weekend Television: Part-time work and flexi-time are commonly arranged.

Lothian Health Board: Jobsharing.

McDonalds: Part-time work has spread to management.

Mars: Reduced hours of up to 6 months, career breaks.

Medilec: Jobsharing, part-time work or reduced hours for returners.

Middlesex Polytechnic: Jobsharing.

Midland Bank: Career break (2 tier) which offers flexible working patterns.

NALGO: Jobshares, flexi-time.

National Westminster Bank: Career breaks (2 tier) with part-time options.

Nationwide Anglia: Career breaks for managers and potential managers; flexi-time plus some part-time work.

North Bedfordshire Health Authority: Jobsharing.

Norwich Union: Career breaks, term-time working, flexible hours.

Ove Arup: Career breaks, flexible working including working from home.

Oxfam: Jobsharing.

Oxford County Council: Jobshare, reduced hours.

Post Office: Jobsharing or part-time work at management discretion.

Prudential Corporation: Career breaks, flexi-time, part-time working widespread; some working from home, term-time and annual hours contracts.

Rank Hovis McDougal (RHM): Part-time work or reduced hours for returners.

Reading Borough Council: Reduced hours, jobsharing.

Research & Development Services: Part-time work, flexi-time, working from home for proportion of working week.

Rists: Part-time work or reduced hours for returners.

Royal Bank of Scotland: Career breaks which include part-time working.

Royal Borough of Kingston Upon Thames: Part-time work, jobsharing, flexi-time, some term-time working.

Royal Insurance: Career breaks open to higher-grade staff.

Rumbelows: Some part-time for returners.

Sainsbury's: Career breaks with flexible hours and pilot term-time working.

Save The Children Fund: Jobsharing, reduced hours.

Sheffield City Council: Career breaks, jobshares, part-time work, flexi-time.

Shell: Career break, jobsharing, part-time work, some working from home.

Sun Alliance: Career breaks.

Sun Life: Career breaks, some flexible working.

Sun Life of Canada: Jobshares, flexible hours.

TSB: Jobshares, flexible hours, career breaks.

Thames Television: Jobshares, part-time work, flexi-time.

Thistle Hotels: Term-time contracts.

TSB: Career breaks, jobsharing.

Tyne Tees Television: Part-time

work or reduced hours for returners.

Unilever: Career break limited to management staff.

United Biscuits: Career break.

Virgin Retail: Part-time or reduced hours for returners.

LEGAL RIGHTS

There are minimum rights for women that are decreed by law, although the better companies prefer to go much further.

The two key pieces of legislation are the Sex Discrimination Act and the Equal Pay Act.

The Sex Discrimination Act states that a woman must not be treated less favourably than a man. The European Equal Treatment Directive goes slightly further, saying that men and women must be treated equally. This can have many ramifications, including whether a woman who does not qualify for maternity leave can be sacked for being pregnant. A European Draft Directive on Pregnancy does state that a woman cannot be sacked for being pregnant and this could become law throughout the European Community.

The Equal Pay Act has been extended to include equal pay for work of equal value. This means that women should not only be paid the same as men for the same job, but the job they are doing can be compared to a man's job and if it can be shown to have equal but different skills, the pay should up accordingly. The eventual effect of the Act should be to eradicate women's low-pay ghettos. The pioneering case for this was when a cook at Cammel Laird Shipyards won the right to be paid the same as male painters.

The Equal Pay Act is mirrored in Article 119 of the Treaty of Rome which maintains the principle that men and women receive equal pay for equal work. Europe leads the way on rights for women – our rights and benefits in this country are considerably less than most of the other EEC countries. There are two other draft directives which if they become law will benefit many women.

The Draft Directive on Part-time Working guarantees part-time workers pro rata benefits of staff who are employed full-time. The Draft Directive on Parental Leave states that either parent is entitled to three months leave for up to two years after the birth of a child. This is on top of maternity leave.

STATUTORY MATERNITY LEAVE AND PAY

Any woman who has been at work for two years eleven weeks
before the baby is born is entitled to Statutory Maternity Pay and
Leave and to return to work. There are two rates of SMP. The
higher rate is 90 per cent of the salary and is payable for the first
six weeks of leave. The lower rate is set by the government (in
April 1991 it was £44.50 per week) and is payable for a maximum
of 18 weeks. You are allowed up to 29 weeks off after the birth of
a child by law.